民航广播词实务
Civil Aviation Broadcasting Practice

主　编　朱林莉
参　编　王　卓　朱　琨　张笔觅
　　　　马丽娜　倪　明　邹海天

北京理工大学出版社
BEIJING INSTITUTE OF TECHNOLOGY PRESS

内 容 提 要

本书共十个模块，分为机场地面服务广播部分和客舱服务广播部分。机场地面服务广播部分由登机前广播（Pre-boarding Announcement）、催促登机广播（Final Boarding Announcement）、航班延误广播（Flight Delay Announcement）和登机口变更广播（Gate Changing Announcement）四个模块组成。客舱服务广播部分由登机广播（Boarding Announcement）、关闭舱门广播（Cadin Door Closing Announcement）、安全演示广播（Safety Demonstration）、起飞广播（Take-off Announcement）、飞机下降广播（Descent Announcement）以及紧急降落广播（Emergency Landing Announcement）六个模块组成。各模块由学习目标、主题引导、快速阅读、专业术语识读、语音训练、主题广播词双语训练、头脑风暴、练习检测、延伸阅读等板块组成。

本书可供高等院校相关专业的学生使用，也可供旅游从业者、民航从业人员作为广播词训练材料使用。

版权专有　侵权必究

图书在版编目（CIP）数据

民航广播词实务 / 朱林莉主编.--北京：北京理工大学出版社，2022.8
ISBN 978-7-5763-1630-8

Ⅰ.①民… Ⅱ.①朱… Ⅲ.①民用航空－乘务人员－英语－口语－高等学校－教材　Ⅳ.①F560.9

中国版本图书馆CIP数据核字（2022）第153437号

出版发行 / 北京理工大学出版社有限责任公司
社　　址 / 北京市海淀区中关村南大街5号
邮　　编 / 100081
电　　话 /（010）68914775（总编室）
　　　　　（010）82562903（教材售后服务热线）
　　　　　（010）68944723（其他图书服务热线）
网　　址 / http：//www.bitpress.com.cn
经　　销 / 全国各地新华书店
印　　刷 / 河北鑫彩博图印刷有限公司
开　　本 / 787毫米×1092毫米　1/16
印　　张 / 10.5　　　　　　　　　　　　　　　责任编辑 / 李　薇
字　　数 / 166千字　　　　　　　　　　　　　文案编辑 / 李　薇
版　　次 / 2022年8月第1版　2022年8月第1次印刷　责任校对 / 周瑞红
定　　价 / 85.00元　　　　　　　　　　　　　责任印制 / 王美丽

图书出现印装质量问题，请拨打售后服务热线，本社负责调换

前言

由于民航行业鲜明的国际化特征，具备良好的民航英语交际技能已是民航服务人员不可或缺的一种职业素质，它直接关系到对客服务的质量，影响到良好民航企业形象的树立。

当前，面对新时代新形势新发展及广大旅客对于美好旅行体验的诉求，航空公司和机场必须不断提高服务旅客广播的质量。目前很多航班的机上广播十分人性化，服务水平越来越高，广播用语大都能做到准确、规范，既专业又通俗易懂。但是也存在一些不足。比如部分机上英文广播词说得磕磕绊绊，这不仅给旅客带来不愉悦之感，更影响了信息的传递。因此，在开设民航相关院校的课程中，增设民航广播词的专项内容非常必要。

本书共十个模块，分为机场地面服务广播部分和客舱服务广播部分。机场地面服务广播部分由登机前广播（Pre-boarding Announcement）、催促登机广播（Final Boarding Announcement）、航班延误广播（Flight Delay Announcement）和登机口变更广播（Gate Changing Announcement）四个模块组成。客舱服务广播部分由登机广播（Boarding Announcement）、关闭舱门广播（Cadin Door Closing Announcement）、安全演示广播（Safety Demonstration）、起飞广播（Takeoff Announcement）、飞机下降广播（Descent Announcement）以及紧急降落广播（Emergency Landing Announcement）六个模

块组成。各模块由学习目标、主题引导、快速阅读、专业术语识读、语音训练、主题广播词双语训练、头脑风暴、练习检测、延伸阅读等板块组成。

本书具有以下特点：

（1）紧贴岗位需求。教材内容注重与民航企业岗位对接，精心挑选民航广播词，符合高等院校培养目标。

（2）注重基础。本书以语音基础知识的学习为开端，在编写过程中进行了大量的前期调研和实践，语音知识呈现通俗易懂，练习难度适宜。

（3）注重趣味性。本书每一模块精心设计并配备广播词展示动画，使学生融入情景中，寓教于乐，便于模仿。情景动画以二维码形式穿插在书中，读者只要用微信扫一扫，即可随时观看学习。

本书由吉林省经济管理干部学院朱林莉担任主编，王卓、朱琨、张笔觅、马丽娜、倪明、邹海天参与本书编写，另外，吉林机场集团地服分公司经理李淼、吉林机场集团地服分公司候机员徐博和韩欣润为本书的编写提供了宝贵的意见。本书在编写过程中得到北京理工大学出版社编辑以及同行的大力支持，并参阅了大量相关资料，在此表示真诚的谢意。

由于编者水平有限，书中难免存在不足之处，敬请读者多提宝贵意见。

编　者

目 录
CONTENTS

Part Ⅰ Airport Ground Service Announcement ········ **001**

    Module 1   Pre-boarding Announcement ·· 003

    Module 2   Final Boarding Announcement ·· 011

    Module 3   Flight Delay Announcement ··· 021

    Module 4   Gate Changing Announcement ··· 031

Part Ⅱ Cabin Service Announcement ···················· **041**

    Module 5   Boarding Announcement ··· 043

    Module 6   Cabin Door Closing Announcement ·································· 052

    Module 7   Safety Demonstration ··· 063

    Module 8   Take-off Announcement ·· 074

    Module 9   Descent Announcement ·· 084

    Module 10   Emergency Landing Announcement ·································· 092

Attachment 1   Cabin Announcement with Phonetic Symbols ············· 101

Attachment 2   The World Leading Airlines ································· 113

Attachment 3   The World Leading Airports ································ 133

References ·· 162

Part I

Airport Ground Service Announcement

Module 1   Pre-boarding Announcement

Module 2   Final Boarding Announcement

Module 3   Flight Delay Announcement

Module 4   Gate Changing Announcement

Part I　Airport Ground Service Announcement

Module 1　Pre-boarding Announcement

Learning Objective

In this module, you will be able to

1. Understand the meaning of English Phonetic Symbols;

2. Use the pronunciati on skills of English Phonetic Symbols while reading;

3. Read the announcement of pre-boarding;

4. Be dedicated to aviation serving.

视频：登机前广播

Guided Learning

Pre-boarding announcement is usually used for reminding the passengers of boarding shortly.

Section A　Warm-up

Ⅰ. Answering the following questions.

1. Can you speak out the name of each picture?
2. Do you know something about them?

Fig.1-1　Airlines

Ⅱ. Find the definition in Column B which matches the word or phrase in Column A.

A	B
1. Chengdu Airlines	a. 春秋航空
2. Spring Airlines	b. 上海航空公司
3. Shanghai Airlines	c. 山东航空公司
4. Shandong Airlines	d. 成都航空

Section B　Phonetic Training

英语音标

英语音标（English Phonetic Symbols）是标记英语读音的符号（像汉语拼音是标记汉字读音的符号一样），用于规范英语口语的发音。在英语字典上音标符号用于标记一个单词的读音，一本英语字典中这些用于标记单词读音的符号被称为英语音标。因此，学习英语音标就是在学习英语发音，学好英语音标是学好标准英语口语的关键，也是有效地帮助我们记忆单词拼写的方法。

英语的发音是由元音和辅音联结成音节形成英语单词的发音，见表 1-1。英式音标有 20 个元音，包括 12 个单元音，8 个双元音。12 个单元音中有 /i:/、/ɜ:/、/u:/、/ɔ:/、/ɑ:/ 5个长元音，其他7个为短元音；28 个辅音，包括 6 个爆破音、10 个摩擦音、6 个破擦音、3 个鼻音、1 个舌侧音、2 个半元音。按照发声时声带是否振动又分为 11 个清辅音和 17 个浊辅音。

表 1-1　DJ 英语国际音标表

元音	单元音	前元音	/i:/	/ɪ/	/e/	/æ/	
		中元音		/ɜ:/	/ə/	/ʌ/	
		后元音	/u:/	/ʊ/	/ɔ:/	/ɒ/	/ɑ:/
	双元音	合口双元音	/eɪ/	/aɪ/	/ɔɪ/	/aʊ/	/əʊ/
		集中双元音	/ɪə/	/eə/	/ʊə/		
辅音	爆破音	清辅音	/p/	/t/	/k/		
		浊辅音	/b/	/d/	/g/		
	摩擦音	清辅音	/f/	/s/	/ʃ/	/θ/	/h/
		浊辅音	/v/	/z/	/ʒ/	/ð/	/r/
	破擦音	清辅音	/tʃ/	/tr/	/ts/		
		浊辅音	/dʒ/	/dr/	/dz/		
	鼻音	（浊辅音）	/m/	/n/	/ŋ/		
	舌侧音	（浊辅音）	/l/				
	半元音	（浊辅音）	/j/	/w/			

注：不同英语词典有不同的音标符号系统，本表为最新 DJ 英语国际音标符号，蓝色为新版音标符号与老版不同。

Section C　Announcement Learning

Setting: It is 17:00 p.m. Jill, a staff of ground service, is standing at the gate to remind the passengers to make preparations for boarding shortly.

Pre-boarding Announcement

Good afternoon, passengers. This is the pre-boarding announcement for flight 898F to Paris. We are now inviting those passengers with small children, and any passengers requiring special assistance to begin boarding at this time. Please have your boarding pass and identification ready. Regular boarding will begin in approximately ten minutes time. Thank you.

登机前广播

各位乘客，下午好！这是飞往巴黎的898F次航班登机前的广播。现在请带小孩的乘客以及需要特别帮助的乘客可以开始登机。请准备好您的登机牌和身份证，大约10分钟后将开始常规登机。谢谢！

Vocabulary and Expressions

special /ˈspeʃ(ə)l/ *adj.* 特别的

assistance /əˈsɪstəns/ *n.* 帮助

boarding pass /ˈbɔːdɪŋ pɑːs/ 登机牌

identification /aɪˌdentɪfɪˈkeɪʃn/ *n.* 身份证明

regular /ˈreɡjələ(r)/ *adj.* 规则的，定期的

approximately /əˈprɒksɪmətli/ /əˈprɑːksɪmətli/ *adv.* 大约

Check your understanding

1. When do you hear this announcement?

2. What do you prepare for boarding?

Tasks

According to sample announcement, make a new announcement by using the prompts given below.

Task 1

Flight Z267, Macao, Good morning

Task 2

Flight A670, Sydney, Good evening

Section D　Progress Check

I. Translate the following phrases and words.

1. 登机前广播

2. 常规登机

3. 特别帮助

4. 登机牌

5. 身份证明

Ⅱ. Translate the following sentences into English.

1. 请准备好您的登机牌和身份证。

2. 大约 10 分钟后将开始常规登机。

3. 这是飞往巴黎的 898F 次航班登机前的广播。

4. 现在请带小孩的乘客以及需要特别帮助的乘客可以开始登机。

Ⅲ. Fill in the blanks according to the text.

1. This is the_____announcement for flight 898F to Paris.

2. We are now_____those passengers with small children, and any passengers requiring_____to begin boarding at this time.

3. Please have your _____ and _____ ready.

4. _____ will begin in _____ ten minutes time.

Further Reading

What Is Checked Baggage?

The term "checked baggage" refers to luggage that is **stowed** in the belly of an **aircraft** during flight. Passengers will leave luggage with **airline** personnel so it can be stowed during flight; this prevents **overcrowding** within the **cabin** of the plane. It **differs from** carry-on baggage, which is any piece of luggage that is carried into the cabin of the airplane for storage in **overhead bins** or underneath seats. Checked baggage **limitations** can **vary**, and many airlines now charge passengers to check a bag onto a flight.

Most airlines require that checked baggage be under a certain weight or size. If the luggage is larger or heavier than the **outlined regulations**, the passenger will be subject to extra fees. In the past, airlines did not charge a fee for bags that fit under the weight and size regulations, but more and more airlines have changed their policies to include fees for checked baggage; many still offer checked bag services free of charge, while others offer free services for one bag only. Fees **apply for** baggage checked beyond the first bag.

  A passenger will check his or her luggage at a **check-in counter** at an airport. Once the bags are checked, they will be **tagged** with the passenger's flight information so the bags can be transferred if the passenger has a **connecting** flight. The bags will be loaded into **storage compartments** in the belly of an airplane by baggage handlers. Once inside the belly of the plane, the bags will be **stacked** and **secured** so they do not **shift** during flight. Passengers will not be able to access checked baggage during flight or at a connecting stop. Once the passenger reaches his or her **final destination**, the luggage will be loaded onto a **conveyor** system that runs into the **baggage claim area** within an airport so the bags can be claimed.

学习总结

Part I　Airport Ground Service Announcement

Module 2　Final Boarding Announcement

Learning Objective

In this module, you will be able to

1. Read the phoneme of monophthong;

2. Use the pronunciation skills of monophthong while reading;

3. Read the announcement of final boarding;

4. Be dedicated to aviation serving.

视频：催促登机广播

Guided Learning

At airport, you hear "final boarding call" announcements. The staff of ground service makes this announcement when almost all of the passengers are on the plane and the gate is about to close.

011

Section A　Warm-up

I. Answering the following questions.

1. Can you speak out the name of each picture?
2. Do you know something about them?

Fig.2-1　Airport Logo

II. Find the definition in Column B which matches the word or phrase in Column A.

A	B
1. Gate	a. 登机办理柜台
2. Airport	b. 航站楼
3. Terminal	c. 机场
4. Check-in	d. 登机口

Section B　Phonetic Training

元音（Vowels）

英语音标中单元音共有 12 个，按照发音长短分为 5 个长元音 /ɑ:/、/ɔ:/、/ɜ:/、/i:/、/u:/ 和 7 个短元音 /ʌ/、/ɒ/、/ə/、/ɪ/、/ʊ/、/e/、/æ/。按照发音时舌面隆起的位置分为 4 个前元音 /i:/、/ɪ/、/e/、/æ/，3 个中元音 /ʌ/、/ɜ:/、/ə/，5 个后元音 /ɔ:/、/ɒ/、/u:/、/ʊ/、/ɑ:/。

1. /ʌ/

发音要领：嘴唇微微张开，伸向两边，舌尖轻触下齿，舌后部稍稍抬起。震动声带，推出气流发出 /ʌ/ 音。

提示：/ʌ/ 为短元音，要诀是发音要短促有力，小腹紧张，注意与 /æ/ 的区别。

绕口令练习：

/ðə ˈkʌstəməz aː əˈkʌstəmd tu ðə dɪsˈgʌstɪŋ ˈkʌstəm/

The customers are accustomed to the disgusting custom.

顾客们习惯了令人讨厌的风俗。

2．/ɒ/

发音要领：口腔打开，嘴张大，舌头向后缩，双唇稍收圆。发音特点是低舌位、后舌位、圆唇。

提示：/ɒ/ 为短元音，发音要短促有力，震动声带发出此音。

绕口令练习：

/ət ðə dɒk aɪm ʃɒkt tu si ðə ˈpɒkɪt ˈrɒkɪt meɪd əv ə blɒk əv rɒk/

At the dock I'm shocked to see the pocket rocket made of a block of rock.

在码头看到一块岩石做的小巧火箭，我感到震惊。

3．/ə/

发音要领：嘴唇微微张开，舌身放平，舌中部稍微抬起，口腔自然放松发声。

提示：发 /ə/ 音时口部肌肉和舌头放松，震动声带，气流向外发出此音。

绕口令练习：

/ən ˈelɪveɪtə ɒn ˈevərɪst ɪz ən ˈevərɪst ˈelɪveɪtə/

An elevator on Everest is an Everest elevator.

珠穆朗玛峰上的电梯是永恒的电梯。

4．/ɪ/

发音要领：嘴唇微微张开，舌尖抵下齿，舌前部抬高，嘴形扁平。声带震动发出声音。

提示：发 /ɪ/ 时要短促有力，像跑步时喊口号"一二一"的"一"音。注意与长元音 /iː/ 的区别。

绕口令练习：

/bɪl wəz ˈbiːtɪŋ ə bɪg biːst wɪð hɪz bɪg fɪst/

Bill was beating a big beast with his big fist.

比尔正用他的大拳头打一头大野兽。

5. /ʊ/

发音要领：嘴唇张开略向前突出，嘴形稍收圆并放松，舌头后缩向软腭抬起，震动声带，短促有力发出 /ʊ/ 音。

提示：/ʊ/ 是短元音，发音时短促有力，收小腹。

绕口令练习：

/gʊd ˈkʊkɪz kʊd biː kʊkt baɪ ə gʊd kʊk, ɪf ə gʊd kʊk kʊd kʊk gʊd ˈkʊkɪz/

Good cookies could be cooked by a good cook, if a good cook could cook good cookies.

如果一位好的厨师能做出美味小甜品的话，那么好吃的小甜品是能够由这位厨师制作出来的。

6. /e/

发音要领：嘴形扁平，舌尖抵下齿，舌前部稍微抬起。发音时下巴逐渐向下移动，震动声带，发出 /e/ 音。

提示：/e/ 个短元音，注意与 /æ/ 的区别。

绕口令练习：

/ˈediz ˈenɪmɪz ˈenvɪd edi ˈenədʒɪ, bʌt edi ˈnevə ˈenvɪd hɪz ˈenɪmɪz ˈenədʒɪ/

Eddie's enemies envied Eddie's energy, but Eddie never envied his enemies' energy.

艾迪的对手羡慕艾迪的精力，但是艾迪从来都不羡慕他对手的精力。

7. /æ/

发音要领：嘴张大，嘴角尽量拉向两边，成扁平形，舌尖抵下齿。尽可能夸张，震动声带，发出 /æ/ 音。

提示：/æ/ 为短元音，发音要干脆利落，要注意与 /e/ 的区别。

绕口令练习：

/kæn jʊ kæn ə kæn æz ə ˈkænə kæn kæn ə kæn/

Can you can a can as a canner can can a can?

你能够像罐头工人一样装罐头吗？

8. /ɑ:/

发音要领：口腔打开，嘴张大，舌身放平，舌尖不抵下齿，下巴放低，放松发音。震动声带，推出气流发出 /ɑ:/ 音，像说："啊"。

提示：/ɑ:/ 是个长元音，注意和短元音 /ʌ/ 的区别。

绕口令练习：

/ðə ʃɑ:ks 'rɪ'mɑ:k ɒn ðə 'mɑ:bl mɑ:k ɪn ðə 'mɑ:kɪt ɪz rɪ'mɑ:kəbl/

The shark's remark on the marble mark in the market is remarkable.
骗子关于市场上大理石标记的评论值得关注。

9. /ɔ:/

发音要领：双唇收得小而圆，并向前突出，舌身往后缩。震动声带，发出 /ɔ:/ 音。

提示：/ɔ:/ 是长元音，发音要与短元音 /ɒ/ 区分。

绕口令练习：

/ju krɔ:s ə krɔ:s ə'krɔ:s ə krɔ:s ɔ: stɪk ə krɔ:s ə'krɔ:s ə krɔ:s/

You cross a cross across a cross,or stick a cross across a cross.
你是跨过一个又一个难关，还是在跨越难关的时候被困住。

10. /ɜ:/

发音要领：嘴形扁平，上下齿微开，舌身平放，舌中部稍稍抬高。震动声带，发出 /ɜ:/ 音。

提示：/ɜ:/ 是长元音，发音要与短元音 /ə/ 区分。要注意的是在美国英语中该音后常常加上一个 r 的音，类似北京方言的儿话音。

绕口令练习：

/aɪ lɜ:n ðæt lɜ:nd 'ɜ:nɪst men ɜ:n mʌtʃ baɪ 'lɜ:nɪŋ/

I learn that learned earnest men earn much by learning.
我得知有学问而认真的人靠学问挣很多钱。

11. /i:/

发音要领：嘴唇微微张开，舌尖抵下齿，嘴角向两边张开，露出微笑的表情，与字母 E 的发音相同。

提示：/i:/ 是长元音，发音的时候要注意与短元音 /i/ 区别。

绕口令练习：

/ə tʃi:p ʃi:p ɪz 'tʃi:pə ðæn ə tʃi:p ʃɪp/

A cheap sheep is cheaper than a cheap ship.

015

一只便宜的绵羊比一艘便宜的船更便宜。

12. /uː/

发音要领：嘴形小而圆，微微外突，舌头尽量后缩。嘴部肌肉是收紧，震动声带，发出 /uː/ 音。

提示：/uː/ 是长元音，发音的时候要注意与短元音 /u/ 区别。

绕口令练习：

/ðə kruː ˌʌnˈskruːd ðə skruːz frɒm ðə ˈsəʊɪŋ məˌʃiːn ənd tʃuːd ðəm/

The crew unscrewed the screws from the sewing-machine and chewed them.

船员们从缝纫机上旋下螺钉并咀嚼它们。

Section C　Announcement Learning

Setting: It is 9 a.m. Amy, a staff of ground service, is standing at the gate to make the final boarding.

Final Boarding Announcement

Hello. This is the final boarding call for passengers Morris and Lorry booked on flight 778Z to Hongkong. Please proceed to gate 6 immediately. The final checks are being completed and the captain will order for the doors of the aircraft to close in approximately five minutes. I repeat. This is the final boarding call for Morris and Lorry. Thank you.

催促登机广播

您好！这是最后一次登机通知。乘客 Morris 和 Lorry 您好，您预订的飞往香港的 778Z 航班，请立即前往 6 号登机口，最后一次的登机查验即将完毕。机长将在 5 分钟内下令关闭飞机舱门。再次提醒！这是最后一次对乘客 Morris 和 Lorry 的登机通知广播。谢谢！

Vocabulary and Expressions

final /ˈfaɪn(ə)l/ *adj.* 最后的

book /bʊk/ *v.* 预订

proceed /prə'si:d/ *v.* 进行

complete /kəm'pli:t/ *v.* 完成

repeat /rɪ'pi:t/ *v.* 重复

immediately /ɪ'mi:diətli/ *adv.* 立刻

Check your understanding

1. Who will make an order for closing the door of aircraft?

2. Which gate should Morris and Lorry for boarding?

Tasks

According to sample announcement, make a new announcement by using the prompts given below.

Task 1

747A, gate 32, captain, New York

Task 2

787A, gate 20, Sam and Sally, Shanghai

Section D Progress Check

I. Translate the following phrases and words.

1. 催促登机广播
2. 6 号登机口
3. 机舱门
4. 登机检查
5. 预订

II. Translate the following sentences into English.

1. 机长将在 5 分钟内下令关闭飞机舱门。

2. 这是最后一次对乘客 Morris 和 Lorry 的登机通知广播。

3. 最后一次的登机查验即将完毕。

4. 乘客 Morris 和 Lorry，您预订的飞往香港的 778Z 航班，请立即前往 6 号登机口。

Ⅲ. **Fill in the blanks according to the text.**

This is the___1___boarding call for___2___Morris and Lorry___3___ on flight 778Z to Hongkong. Please___4___to gate 6___5___. The final checks are being___6___and the___7___will order for the doors of the aircraft to___8___in approximately five minutes. I___9___. This is the final boarding call___10___Morris and Lorry.

Further Reading

Getting Mobile Boarding Passes

Now that nearly everyone travels with a smartphone or other **handheld device**, major airlines allow passengers to use those devices to access boarding passes. (Even Southwest's boarding process, which is run differently from other airlines, allows for the use of mobile boarding passes.) Using a mobile boarding pass saves paper and makes it harder to lose the pass. A piece of paper can be **misplaced**, but most people always have their phones **handy**.

Generally, mobile boarding passes are **accessible** starting 24 hours before departure. **Log** onto the airline's website and check in for the flight. Once you're checked in, the site should offer the option to send you a mobile boarding pass by text or email or using the airline's app. It should look similar to a paper boarding pass, right down to a **scannable** bar code.

Before **banking on** using a mobile boarding pass, though, check the airline's website to make sure they're accepted at your airport. Some smaller **regional** airports take longer to get this option set up. Because accessing the boarding pass may require that the holder have internet access—and **technical** issues tend to happen at the **least-convenient** times—take a **screenshot** of the boarding pass and save it to the **images folder** of the phone or tablet. If it's not possible to load the boarding pass when it's time to board, pull up the screenshot and use that instead.

Part I Airport Ground Service Announcement

学习总结

Part I Airport Ground Service Announcement

Module 3 Flight Delay Announcement

Learning Objective

In this module, you will be able to

1. Read the phoneme of diphthongs;

2. Use the pronunciation skills of diphthongs while reading;

3. Read the announcement off light delay;

4. Be dedicated to aviation serving.

视频：航班延误广播

Guided Learning

The airline staff makes this announcement when the aircraft cannot be scheduled for arrival or departure.

Section A Warm-up

I. Answering the following questions.

1. Can you speak out the name of each picture?
2. Do you know something about them?

Fig.3-1   Airport Logo

II. Find the definition in Column B which matches the word or phrase in Column A.

A	B
1. Departure	a. 转机航班
2. Baggage claim	b. 出发
3. Customs control	c. 行李提取处
4. Connecting flights	d. 海关

Section B Phonetic Training

双元音（Diphthongs）

双元音在语音学中，是指联合的两个元音，它们作为一个整体出现。之间有平滑的过渡，也就是说，双元音中的发音牵涉两种不同的舌位，并且从其中一种舌位滑动到另一舌位。双元音音素由两个元音组成，发音时由一个元音向另一个元音滑动，口型有变化。前一个元音发音清晰响亮，且时间长；后一个元音发音模糊软弱，且时间短。特别要注意以下三点：

（1）不要将前后两个音断开，应连贯成为一个整体；

（2）不要因为后一个元音发音短小而将其忽略；

（3）发音时滑动过程要完整，时间要充分。

在英式音标符号中双元音有 /aɪ/、/eɪ/、/aʊ/、/əʊ/、/ɔɪ/、/ɪə/、/eə/、/ʊə/8 个，而在美式音标中只有 [aɪ]、[ɔɪ]、[aʊ]3 个双元音符号。8 个英式音标中的双元音按照口型可归纳为如下 3 组。

1. /ɪ/ 音组：/eɪ/、/aɪ/、/ɔɪ/。

（1）/eɪ/。发音要领：由 /e/ 和 /ɪ/ 两个元音组成，嘴巴张开成半圆形，开始发 /e/ 音，然后颚部慢慢抬起滑向 /ɪ/ 音，嘴唇慢慢合上。与字母 A 的读音相同。

提示：/eɪ/ 发音时音量从强到弱，前长后短，前重后轻。

绕口令练习：

/ðə leɪs pleɪst ɪn ðə 'pælɪs ɪz rɪ'pleɪst 'fɜːst, ənd dɪs'pleɪst leɪt/

The lace placed in the palace is replaced first, and displaced late.

放在皇宫的带子先被替换，随后被转移。

（2）/aɪ/。发音要领：由 /a/ 和 /ɪ/ 两个元音组成，双唇张开，开始发 /ɑː/ 音，舌部肌肉放松，然后颚部慢慢抬起滑向 /ɪ/ 音，嘴唇慢慢合上。与字母 I 的读音相同。

提示：/aɪ/ 发音时舌位由低到高，音量由强到弱，由长到短，由清晰到含糊。

绕口令练习：

/aɪ laɪk tu raɪd maɪ laɪt waɪt baɪk ənd flaɪ ə waɪt laɪt kaɪt wɪð maɪ waɪf/

I like to ride my light white bike ,and fly a white light kite with my wife.

我喜欢和我的妻子骑着白色的轻便自行车放白色的轻风筝。

（3）/ɔɪ/。发音要领：舌身放松前探，舌尖轻触下齿，舌前部微微抬起。整个过程就是从 /ɔː/ 音慢慢滑向 /ɪ/。

提示：/ɔɪ/ 发音时舌位由低到高，由舌后部抬高滑向舌前部抬高，音量由强到弱，由长到短，由清晰到含糊。

绕口令练习：

/bɔɪl ðiː ɔɪl sɔɪld baɪ ðə kɔɪl ɪn ðə 'tɔɪlɪt lest ɪt spɔːɪl/

Boil the oil soiled by the coil in the toilet lest it spoil.

把被盥洗室里的线圈弄脏的油煮开，免得它变质。

2. /ʊ/ 音组：/aʊ/、/əʊ/。

（1）/aʊ/。发音要领：由 /a/ 和 /ʊ/ 两个元音组成，先发 /a/ 音，然后嘴巴收圆合拢，舌尖离开下齿，舌身后缩，舌后部向软腭抬起，发音慢慢滑向 /ʊ/。

提示：/aʊ/ 音量由强到弱，由长到短，由清晰到含糊。

绕口令练习：

/ðə haʊnd faʊnd ə prəˈfaʊnd bʊk ɒn ðə ˈraʊndəbaʊt/

The hound found a profound book on the roundabout.

猎犬在旋转木马上找到一本深奥的书。

（2）/əʊ/。发音要领：由 /ə/ 和 /ʊ/ 两个元音组成，先发 /ə/ 音，然后很快的滑向 /ʊ/ 音，发音结束时，颚部慢慢抬起，嘴唇慢慢合上。

提示：/əʊ/ 发音时口型由略微呈圆形较大到收圆缩小，音量由强到弱，该音是字母"o"的读音。

绕口令练习：

/ðə ˈsəʊldʒəz ˈʃəʊldəd ˈʃuːtəz ɒn ðeə ˈʃəʊldəz/

The soldiers shouldered shooters on their shoulders.

战士肩背着枪。

3. /ə/ 音组：/ɪə/、/eə/、/ʊə/

（1）/ɪə/。发音要领：由 /ɪ/ 和 /ə/ 两个元音组成。首先发短 /ɪ/ 的音，然后很快的滑向 /ə/ 音，发音过程中口型始终是半开的。

提示：/ɪə/ 前一个成分要短一些，模糊一点，而后一个成分要长一些，清晰一点。英式音标中 /ə/ 要扁平，没有卷舌音。

绕口令练习：

/aɪ ʃed teəz fə hi ʃɪəz maɪ dɪə tɔɪ dɪəz ɪə/

I shed tears for he shears my dear toy deer's ear.

我流泪是因为他剪掉了我心爱的玩具鹿的耳朵。

（2）/eə/。发音要领：由 /e/ 和 /ə/ 两个元音组成。首先发前元音 /e/，同时舌尖轻触下齿，然后很快滑向 /ə/ 音，发音过程中双唇半开。

提示：/eə/ 是个"集中双元音"，发音 /e/ 时嘴角向两边拉，滑向 /ə/ 音收小，口型由大变小。

绕口令练习：

/aɪ met ə ˈfeəlɪ ˌʌnˈfeə əˈfeə ˌʌpˈsteəz/

I met a fairly unfair affair upstairs.

我在楼上遇到一件颇不公平的事。

（3）/ʊə/。发音要领：由 /ʊ/ 和 /ə/ 两个元音组成。首先发 /ʊ/ 的音，然后慢慢滑向 /ə/ 的音即可，口型由收圆变化为最后半开。

提示：/ʊə/ 前强后弱，英式发音发 /ə/ 部分不卷舌，美式发音卷舌。

绕口令练习：

/aɪ əˈʃʊə ðə ˈɪndʒəd ˈdʒʊərɪ ðæt ə ʃʊə ɪnˈʃʊərəns ɪz ɪnˈʃʊəd/

I assure the injured jury that a sure insurance is ensured.

我向受伤的陪审团保证一笔有把握的保险已被担保。

Section C Announcement Learning

Setting: It is 9 a.m. Amy, a flight attendant, is making the announcement for flight delay.

Flight Delay Announcement

Ladies and gentlemen, can I have your attention please?

We regret to inform you that a thunderstorm in Seattle has delayed several flights. Flight 797F to Shanghai, scheduled for departure at 8:30 from gate A, is now scheduled to depart at 10:35 from gate F. Please check the arrivals and departure boards, located on the concourses of each main terminal, for more specific information and updates on individual flights. We are sorry for the inconvenience.

延误广播

女士们、先生们，请注意：

我们抱歉的通知，西雅图的一场雷雨延误了几个航班。飞往上海的797F航班原定于8：30从A登机口起飞，现在定于10：35从F登机口起飞。请查看位于候机大厅的到达和起飞电子公告牌，了解有关航班的具体信息和最新动态。给您带来不便，在此，我们深表歉意。

Vocabulary and Expression

inform /ɪnˈfɔːm/ v. 通知

schedule /ˈʃedjuːl/ *v.* 计划，安排

departure /dɪˈpɑːtʃə(r)/ *v.* 出发，启程

concourse /ˈkɒŋkɔːs/ *n.* 大厅

terminal /ˈtɜːmɪn(ə)l/ *n.* 终点站，航站楼

update /ˌʌpˈdeɪt/ /əpˈdeɪt/ *n.* 最新消息

inconvenience /ˌɪnkənˈviːniəns/ *adj.* 不便利的

Check your understanding

1. Please describe your feelings of experiencing the flight delay.

2. What do you usually do when you are waiting for the delaying fight?

Tasks

According to sample announcement, make a new announcement by using the prompts given below.

Task 1

Flight 109, gate B, storm, Sanya, Changchun

Task 2

Flight 256, gate E, sandstorm, Nanjing, Shenzhen

Section D Progress Check

I. Translate the following phrases and words.

1. 航班延误
2. 最新动态
3. 具体信息
4. 位于
5. 起飞和到达公告牌

II. Translate the following sentences into English.

1. 给您带来不便，在此，我们深表歉意。
2. 请查看位于候机大厅的到达和起飞电子公告牌。
3. 我们抱歉的通知，西雅图的一场雷雨延误了几个航班。
4. 飞往上海的797F 航班现在定于10：35 从 F 登机口起飞。

III. Fill in the blanks according to the text.

We ___1___ to inform you that a thunderstorm in Seattle has ___2___ several flights. Flight 797F to Shanghai, scheduled for ___3___ at 8:30 from gate A, is now ___4___ to depart at 10:35 from gate F. Please check the ___5___ and departure boards, ___6___ on the concourses of each main ___7___, for more ___8___ information and updates on ___9___ flights. We are sorry for the ___10___.

Further Reading

Airports in Shanghai Deal with Flight Delays

Strengthening of communication and release of information

Airports in Shanghai have been attending daily information communication meetings organized by air traffic departments to understand airspace flow control information as well as information concerning flight dispatch, which has allowed them to provide precise information forecasts to seize interval airspace and dispatch as many flights as possible.

Airports in Shanghai have been giving full play to the role as a one-stop air travel platform, actively communicating with air traffic control departments, airlines and other board members to retrieve relative information in time. They are continuously releasing flow control warnings, dynamic information about airport operations as well as flight delays and cancellations via the official "One-Stop Air Travel—Airports" microblog, reminding passengers to pay attention to flight changes and make reasonable travel arrangements. The airports are also interacting with passengers through private messages to reduce anxiety.

In nearly half a month, the micro-blogging platform of "One-Stop Air Travel—Airports in Shanghai" has sent many push notifications regarding delay warnings and reminders for typhoons and traffic. The airports have also provided passengers with information through WeChat's online flight inquiry function. They have launched a live broadcast and hotline mechanism between airport operations control and the News Center of Radio and

Television Shanghai to broadcast dynamic news concerning airport operation.

Strengthening on-site control of terminals

Large-scale flight delays have put great pressure on on-site control of airports. Airports in Shanghai have launched a linked emergency response mechanism regarding the extent of delays and strengthened on-site service and control strength, avoiding overcrowding and maintaining order.

Passengers may have to go through security multiple times due to flight delays, so airports have communicated with airline staff to get first hand information and avoid crowds.

Airports have also launched a combined service force and linkage mechanism according to the real-time situation and adjusted security checkpoints in a reasonable manner.

Strengthening of communication, business, transportation and other service support

To provide services and support to stranded passengers, Pudong and Hongqiao International Airport have introduced many people-oriented services and initiatives to ensure sufficient business and catering services in terminal buildings.

For instance, Hongqiao International Airport has started to provide "authentication without notice" service for Wi-Fi access, which has enhanced the web surfing experience of stranded passengers. Staff in the terminal areas have been providing on-site interactive activities for passengers with kids. Commercial departments of airports have organized summer-themed promotion of delicacies, discounts of well-known brands and other activities, reducing the anxiety and exhaustion of passengers who are delayed.

Large-scale flight delays and cancellations have led to a sharp increase in the number of flights landing at the airports at night. Since subway lines and bus routes are out of service after 11:00 p.m, transportation for passengers at night has become a difficulty.

学习总结

Part I Airport Ground Service Announcement

Module 4　Gate Changing Announcement

Learning Objective

In this module, you will be able to

1. Read the phoneme of consonants;

2. Use the pronunciation skills of consonants while reading;

视频：登机口变更广播

3. Read the announcement of changing boarding gate;

4. Be dedicated to aviation serving.

Guided Learning

Gate changing announcement is usually used for informing the passengers the boarding gate is changed, and make preparations for boarding in advance.

Section A Warm-up

I. Answering the following questions.

1. Can you speak out the name of each picture?
2. Do you know something about them?

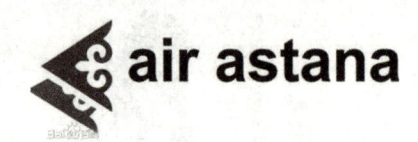

Fig.4-1　International Airlines

II. Find the definition in Column B which matches the word or phrase in Column A.

A	B
1. Air Astana	a. 阿联酋航空
2. Druk air-Royal Bhutan Airlines	b. 巴基斯坦航空
3. Emirates Airlines	c. 不丹皇家航空公司
4. Pakistan International Airlines	d. 阿斯塔纳航空

Section B Phonetic Training

辅音（Consonants）

气流在口腔或咽喉受到阻碍而形成的音叫作辅音。辅音发音时气流受到发音器官的各种阻碍，声带不一定振动，不够清晰响亮。标记辅音的符号叫作辅音音标。国际英语中共有 28 个辅音音标。

清辅音：/p/ /t/ /k/ /f/ /s/ /θ/ /h/ /ʃ/ /tʃ/ /tr/ /ts/
浊辅音：/b/ /d/ /g/ /v/ /z/ /ð/ /ʒ/ /r/ /dʒ/ /dr/ /dz/ /m/ /n/ /ŋ/ /l/ /w/ /j/

1. /p/

发音要领：双唇紧闭，然后快速张开，让气流冲出口腔，发出爆破音，但声带不振动。

提示：/p/ 是个清辅音，声带不震动，产生的声音不是声带而是气流，要注意与 /b/ 的区别。

绕口令：

/ə 'pleznt 'peznt ki:ps ə 'pleznt 'feznt/

A pleasant peasant keeps a pleasant pheasant.

一位和善的农民养了一只讨人喜欢的野鸡。

2. /b/

发音要领：双唇紧闭，然后快速张开，让气流冲出口腔，发出爆破音，但声带需振动。

提示：/b/ 是个浊辅音，声带震动发声。在 /b/ 后面添加元音 /ə/，例如把 cab/kæb/ 错发成 /kæbə/、/kæp/，这些问题应在平时练习时多加注意。

绕口令：

/'beɪbɪ 'bɒbɪ ənd 'beɪbɪ 'bɪlɪ laɪk bʊks, bʌt 'əʊnlɪ 'beɪbɪ 'bɪlɪ weəz bu:ts/

Baby Bobby and baby Billy like books, but only baby Billy wears boots.

宝贝鲍比和宝贝比利喜欢图书，但仅宝贝比利穿靴子。

Section C　Announcement Learning

Setting: It is 3 p.m. Amy, a staff of ground service, is standing at the gate to remind the passengers of making preparations for boarding gate changing.

Fig.4-2 Descent

Gate Changing Announcement

Hello. Passengers of flight 571A bound for Auckland, with stops in Guanghzou, the departure gate has been changed to 17G. Also, there will be a slight departure delay due to inclement weather outside. The ground crew is in the process of deicing the wings in preparation for departure. Thank you for your patience.

登机口更改广播

乘坐571A航班飞往奥克兰经停广州的乘客，您好！您所乘坐航班的登机口已改为17G。此外，由于恶劣天气影响，出发将略有延误。机场地勤工作人员正在为飞机起飞进行除冰作业。感谢您的理解！

Vocabulary and Expressions

bound for /baʊnd fː(r)/ 飞往
slight /slaɪt/ adj. 略微的
inclement /ɪnˈklemənt/ adj. 恶劣的
ground crew /graʊnd kruː/ 地勤人员
process /ˈprəʊses/ n. 过程
deice /ˌdiːˈaɪs/ v. 除冰

Check your understanding

1. Why did the fight have a slight departure delay?

2. What did the crew prepare for departure?

Tasks

According to sample announcement, make a new announcement by using the prompts given below.

Task 1

Kunming , flight BW27, gate 20

Task 2

Berlin, flight CA88, gate 22

Section D Progress Check

I. Translate the following phrases and words.

1. 奥克兰
2. 恶劣天气
3. 登机口
4. 机组人员
5. 由于

II. Translate the following sentences into English.

1. 由于恶劣天气影响，出发将略有延误。
2. 机场地勤工作人员正在为飞机起飞进行除冰作业。
3. 乘坐571A航班飞往奥克兰经停广州的乘客，您好！您所乘坐航班的登机口已改为17G。
4. 感谢您的理解。

III. Fill in the blanks according to the text.

1. Passengers of flight 571A_____Auckland, with stops in Guanghzou, the departure gate has_____changed to 17G.

2. Also, there will be a_____departure delay_____inclement weather outside.

3. The_____crew is in the process of_____the wings in preparation for departure.

4. Thank you for your_____.

Further Reading

What to Do if Your Flight Is Disrupted

Get the Latest Information

In the case of flight disruptions, we will provide regular updates to our customers. Please check the Travel alerts posted on the homepage for the latest updates. You can also check Flight status on our website.

If you are already at the airport, you can check the latest updates via the screens or public announcements. Cathay Pacific airport agents are always there for assistance.

Provide Contact Information

Please ensure that your contact information is accurate within Manage booking, to receive the latest updates. Customers can sign up for *notification* mobile text messages (SMS), to be alerted of changes to flight status. This is especially helpful when internet access is not available. Note that, if you change your mobile phone SIM card while travelling, *notification* text messages will not be delivered.

Manage Your Booking

Subject to the nature of the flight cancellation, we will issue special ticketing guidelines ahead of a flight disruption allowing for passengers to make changes to their booking free of charge.

Customers who booked via Cathay Pacific. com or Cathay Pacific mobile app, who wish to change their travel arrangements, may do so via Manage booking, subject to the special ticketing guidelines issued for your flight rebooking–the guidelines will be linked to from the Travel alert when available.

Customers who booked through a travel agent should contact their booking agent for assistance first.

If your flight is canceled, or missed due to disruption delay, we'll do our best to automatically rebook you onto the next available flight, within the same cabin originally purchased. Your new flight details will be reflected within Manage booking. Note that, if the number of affected customers is particularly high, we may take time to process your new travel arrangements.

Before You Go to the Airport

If you receive information that your flight has been delayed or cancelled, please do not proceed to the airport for the originally scheduled flight.

If your flight has been delayed, and there is a new estimated time of departure, the check-in and boarding times will reflect the new departure time.

If your flight has been cancelled and you have a new flight arrangement, please note the new check-in and boarding times.

In circumstances where flight disruptions are due to local weather, we suggest checking with your local transportation options on any delays or cancellations that may affect your journey to the airport.

学习总结

Part I Airport Ground Service Announcement

民航广播词实务
Civil Aviation Broadcasting Practice

Part II
Cabin Service Announcement

Module 5　　Boarding Announcement

Module 6　　Cabin Door Closing Announcement

Module 7　　Safety Demonstration

Module 8　　Take-off Announcement

Module 9　　Descent Announcement

Module 10　 Emergency Landing Announcement

Part II   Cabin Service Announcement

Module 5   Boarding Announcement

Learning Objective

In this module, you will be able to

1. Read the phoneme of plosive;

2. Use the pronunciation skills of incomplete explosion while reading;

3. Read the announcement during Boarding;

4. Be dedicated to aviation serving.

视频：登机广播

Guided Learning

Boarding announcement is usually made while the aircraft is parked at the gate and the last passengers are boarding.

043

Section A Warm-up

I. Read the following pictures and answer the questions.

1. Can you speak out the name of each picture?
2. Could you please say something about them?

Fig.5-1   Airlines Logo

II. Find the definition in Column B which matches the word or phrase in Column A.

A	B
1. China Southern Airlines	a. 中国海南航空
2. China Eastern Airlines	b. 中国国际航空
3. Air China	c. 中国南方航空
4. Hainan Airlines	d. 中国厦门航空
5. Xiamen Airlines	e. 中国东方航空

Section B Phonetic Training

爆破音（Plosive）

1. /t/

发音要领：舌尖抵上齿龈，憋住气，然后突然弹开舌尖，让气流从口腔喷出，但声带不振动。

提示：不要用汉语拼音中的 t 来代替这个发音。在词尾出现时，千万不要加上一个弱读的元音 /ə/！

绕口令：

/ˈbetɪ' bʊtər bɔːt sʌm 'bʌtə, bʌt ʃiː sed ðə 'bʌtəz 'bɪtə/

Betty Botter bought some butter, but she said the butter's bitter.

贝蒂·波特买了些黄油，但是她说黄油有点苦。

2. /d/

发音要领：舌尖抵上齿龈，憋住气，然后弹开舌尖，让气流从口腔中喷出，但声带需振动。

提示：/d/ 是个浊辅音，声带震动发声。注意与轻辅音 /t/ 的区别。不要用汉语拼音中的 d 来代替，英语发声比较靠后，是由声带震动发声。

绕口令：

/deɪl ðə def dɒg laɪks tu dɪg diːp həʊlz/

Dale the deaf dog likes to dig deep holes.

聋哑狗戴尔喜欢挖深坑。

3. /k/

发音要领：舌后部抵住软腭，憋住气，然后突然间离开，将气送出来，像咳嗽一样，但声带不震动。

提示：/k/ 是个清辅音，声带不震动，产生的声音不是声带而是气流，要注意与 /g/ 的区别。

绕口令：

/bleɪks blæk baɪks bæk breɪk ˈbrækɪt blɒk brəʊk/

Blake's black bike's back brake bracket block broke.

布雷克的黑色自行车的后闸托架垫块坏了。

4. /g/

发音要领：舌后部抵住软腭，憋住气，然后突然间离开，将气送出来，但声带需振动。

提示：/g/ 是个浊辅音，声带震动发声。注意不要用汉语拼音中的 g 来代替，汉语拼音的 g 是口腔发音，音标是声带震动发音。

绕口令：

/ə bɪg blæk bʌg bɪt ə bɪg blæk dɒg ɒn hɪz bɪg blæk nəʊz/

A big black bug bit a big black dog on his big black nose!

一只黑色的大臭虫在一只大黑狗的黑色鼻子上咬了一口。

Section C　Announcement Learning

Setting: It is 13:00 p.m. On Thursday. Passengers are boarding the aircraft. Amy, a flight attendant, is making boarding announcement to welcome passengers.

Boarding Announcement

Ladies and gentlemen, the Captain has turned on the Fasten Seat Belt sign. If you haven't already done so, please stow your carry-on luggage **underneath** the seat in front of you or in an **overhead bin**. Please take your seat and fasten your seat belt. And also make sure your seat back and folding trays are in their full upright position.

If you are seated next to an **emergency exit**, please read carefully the special instructions card located by your seat. If you do not wish to perform the functions described in the event of an emergency, please ask a flight attendant to reseat you.

We remind you that this is a **non-smoking flight**. Smoking is prohibited on the entire aircraft, including the lavatories. Tampering with, disabling or destroying the lavatory **smoke detectors** is prohibited by law.

登机广播

女士们、先生们，机长已经打开安全带指示灯。如果您尚未这样做，请将随身行李存放在您前面的座位下方或头顶行李箱中。请系好安全带。还要确保您的座椅靠背和折叠托盘处于完全直立的位置。

如果您坐在紧急出口旁边，请仔细阅读座位旁边的特别说明卡。如果您不希望在紧急情况下执行描述的功能，请让乘务员重新为您准备座位。

我们提醒您，这是一个禁烟航班。整个飞机（包括厕所）禁止吸烟。法律禁止篡改、禁用或毁坏厕所烟雾探测器。

Vocabulary and Expressions

captain /ˈkæptɪn/ *n.* 机长

stow /stəʊ/ *v.* 把……收好

Seat Belt sign /siː t belt saɪn/ 安全带提示信号灯

carry-on luggage /ˈkæri-ɒn ˈlʌgɪdʒ/ 随身携带行李

underneath /ˌʌndərˈniθ/ prep. 在下方

overhead bin /ˈoʊvərˌhed bɪn/ 头顶储物箱

seat back /siːt bæk/ 座椅靠背

upright position /ˈʌpraɪt pəˈzɪʃən/ 垂直位置

Check your understanding

1. Who is making the announcement?

2. What does he or she is mentioning?

3. Where does the passenger ask to sit?

Tasks

According to sample announcement, make conversations with your partner by using the prompts given below.

Task 1

Boarding announcement, China Southern Airlines, Boeing 787

Task 2

Boarding announcement, China Eastern Airlines, Airbus 350

Task 3

Boarding announcement, Air China, Airbus 380

Section D Progress Check

I. Translate the following phrases and words.

1. 禁烟航班
2. 紧急出口
3. 在……下方
4. 烟雾探测器
5. 头顶行李箱

II. Translate the following sentences into English.

1. 如果您坐在紧急出口旁边，请仔细阅读座位旁边的特别说明卡。

2. 整个飞机（包括厕所）禁止吸烟。

3. 如果您尚未这样做，请将随身行李存放在您前面的座位下方或头顶行李箱中。

4. 我们提醒您，这是一个禁烟航班。

Ⅲ. Fill in the blanks according to the text.

1. The Captain has_____the Fasten Seat Belt sign.

2. If you haven't already done so, please stow your_____underneath the seat in front of you or in an overhead bin.

3. Make sure your seat back and_____are in their full upright position.

4. If you are seated next to an emergency exit, please read carefully the special_____card located by your seat.

Further Reading

Check-in at a Self-service Kiosk

Nearly all airlines have switched to self-service check-in kiosks. If you have never used a self-service check-in kiosk before, here is what you will need to do the next time you go to the airport.

Look for Kiosks at the Airport

When you reach the head of your airline's check-in line, you will see a row of kiosks, which look like free-standing computer screens, instead of a customer service representative.

Your airline will have an employee available to print out your baggage tags and place your bags on the conveyor belt, but you will first need to use a kiosk to check in for your flight.

Identify Yourself

Walk up to an open kiosk, bringing your luggage with you. The kiosk will prompt you to identify yourself, either by inserting a credit card, typing in your flight confirmation code or entering your frequent flyer number. Enter your identifying information using the keyboard shown on the touch screen. You will be able to touch a "clear" or "backspace" key if you make a mistake.

Confirm Flight Information

You should now see a screen which shows your name and air travel itinerary. You will probably be asked to confirm your flight information by touching an "OK" or "Enter" button on the screen.

Choose or Confirm Your Seats

You will be able to review and change your seat assignment during the check-in process.

Be careful some airlines have their seat assignment screen default to a page which will entice you to pay extra to upgrade your seat. If you have swiped a credit card to identify yourself, be sure to skip the seat upgrade option unless you really intend to use it, as the kiosk already has your credit card information.

After you skip the upgrade screen, you can change your seat, provided there are open seats on your flight.

Indicate Whether You Will Be Checking a Bag

If you have already checked in for your flight online, you will probably be able to scan your printed boarding pass at the kiosk. When you scan your boarding pass, the kiosk will identify you and begin the luggage check-in process.

Print and Collect Your Boarding Passes

At this point, the kiosk should begin to print your boarding pass (or passes, if you have a connecting flight).

学习总结

Part II Cabin Service Announcement

Module 6　Cabin Door Closing Announcement

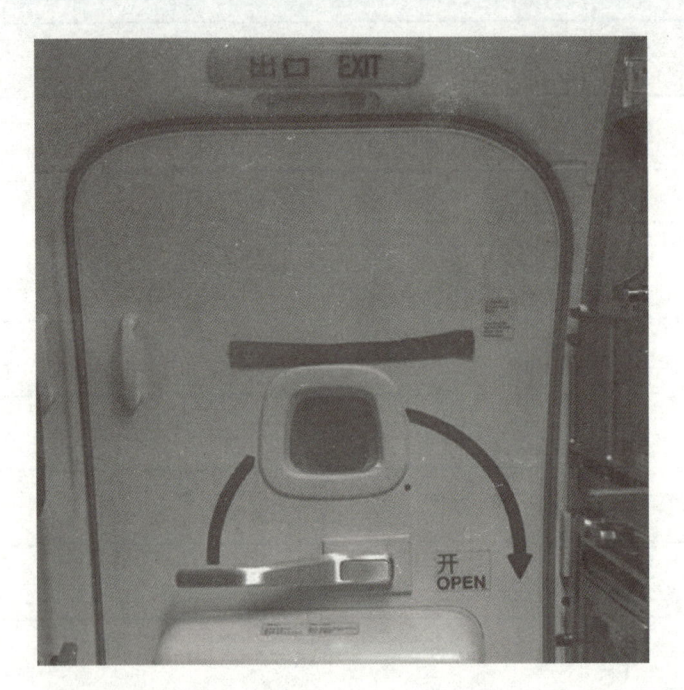

Learning Objective

In this module, you will be able to

1. Read the phonemes of fricative;

2. Use the pronunciation skills of fricatives while reading;

3. Read the announcement of door closure;

4. Be dedicated to aviation serving.

视频：关闭舱门广播

Guided Learning

Usually before the door is closed, or while it is closed, this announcement is made.

Part Ⅱ Cabin Service Announcement

Section A Warm-up

I. Answering the following questions.

1. Can you speak out the name of each picture?
2. Do you know something about them?

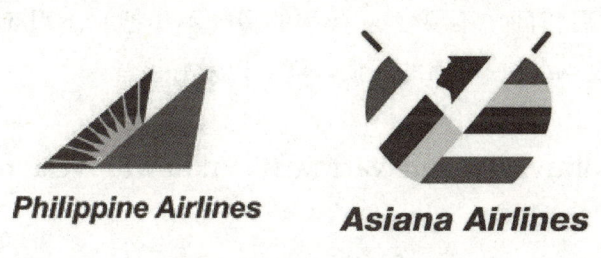

Fig.6-1 International Airlines

II. Find the definition in Column B which matches the word or phrase in Column A.

A	B
1. JC International Airlines	a. 韩亚航空
2. Asiana Airlines	b. 大韩航空
3. Philippine Airlines	c. 柬埔寨国际航空
4. Korean Airlines	d. 菲律宾航空

Section B Phonetic Training

摩擦音（Fricatives）

1. /f/

发音要领：上齿轻轻接触下唇，然后吹气，让气流从唇齿间通过，形成摩擦，但声带不振动。

提示：/f/ 是个清辅音，声带不震动，产生的声音不是声带而是气流，要注意与浊辅音 /v/ 的区别。

绕口令：

/ˈfɪfti faɪv ˈfaɪəˌfaɪtəz ˈfraɪd fɪfti faɪv frentʃ ˈfraɪz/

Fifty-five firefighters fried fifty-five French fries.

五十五名消防人员炸出五十五根薯条。

2. /v/

发音要领：上齿轻轻接触下唇，然后吹气，让气流从唇齿间通过，形成摩擦，但声带需振动。

提示：/v/ 是个浊辅音，声带震动发声。要注意上齿与下唇的咬合，气流通过唇齿间，不要发成 /w/ 的音。不要把 love /lʌv/ 错发成 /lʌw/。只要发 /v/ 养成咬唇的习惯，就可以发好该音。

绕口令：

/ˈVivian draɪvz ðə væn ˈverɪ fɑːst. Vɪkta wəz ˈverɪ ˈnɜːvəs ɪn ðə væn/

Vivian drives the van very fast. Victor was very nervous in the van.

维维安开车很快。维克托在车里很紧张。

3. /s/

发音要领：双唇微微张开，舌头自然放松，气流从上下齿隙间送出，但声带不振动。

提示：/s/ 是个清辅音，声带不震动。要注意与 /ð/、/θ/、/z/ 的区别。

绕口令：

/ɪn ðə ˈpæsɪdʒ ðə ˈpæsɪndʒə pɑːst ə kəˈset əv ˈmesɪdʒ tu ˈmesɪndʒə/

In the passage the passenger passed a cassette of message to messenger.

在过道里，乘客给信差传递了一盒带信息。

4. /z/

发音要领：双唇微微张开，舌头自然放松，气流从上下齿隙间送出，但声带需振动。

提示：/z/ 是个浊辅音，要振动声带发音，气流较强。注意用汉语的"资"来代替 /z/ 的发音是不正确的。

绕口令：

/ðə ˈkreɪzi ˈdʒæzˌmæn geɪzd ət ðə bleɪz ɒn ðə ˈrezə(r) wɪð əˈmeɪzmənt/

The crazy jazzman gazed at the blaze on the razor with amazement.

疯狂的爵士音乐演奏者惊愕地盯着剃刀上的光辉。

5. /ʃ/

发音要领：双唇收圆并稍微突出，舌尖接近上齿龈，送气，声带不振动。

提示：/ʃ/ 是个清辅音，声带不震动。/ʃ/ 和汉语拼音中的声母 sh 很相近，但要注意的是 /ʃ/ 不卷舌，是个平舌音。

绕口令：

/ən ˈɪŋglɪʃ ˈfɪʃəmən ˈwɪʃɪz tu get ə ˈfuːlɪʃ fɪʃ fər ə kəʊld dɪʃ/

An English fisherman wishes to get a foolish fish for a cold dish.

一个英国渔夫希望捕到一条自投罗网的鱼来充饥。

6. /ʒ/

发音要领：双唇收圆并稍微突出，舌头稍微上卷，舌尖接近上齿龈，送气，但声带需振动。

提示：/ʒ/ 是个浊辅音，发音时只有微弱气流泻出，这是一个较难发准的音，要注意声带的震动。

绕口令：

/hiː ˈmeʒəd hɪz ˈpleʒə ɪn ə ˈvɪʒʊəl ˈtreʒə/

He measured his pleasure in a visual treasure.

他用视觉上的珍宝来衡量自己的快乐。

7. /θ/

发音要领：舌尖微微伸出，上下齿轻轻咬住舌尖，送气，但声带不振动。

提示：/θ/ 是个清辅音，声带不震动。要注意与 /ð/、/s/、/z/ 的区别，发这个音主要是舌尖与上齿之间的摩擦，所以千万不要紧紧咬住舌尖，应该是上齿轻触舌尖。

绕口令：

/ˈθɜːti ˈθɜːsti θiːvz θɪŋk ðeə θruː/

Thirty thirsty thieves think they're through.

三十个口渴的小偷认为他们已经渡过了难关。

8. /ð/

发音要领：上下齿轻轻咬住舌尖，送气，但声带需振动。

提示：/ð/ 是舌齿、浊辅音，舌尖和下齿之间的气流通道非常窄小。发这个音主要是舌尖与上齿之间的摩擦，所以千万不要紧紧咬住舌尖，只要轻轻咬一咬就行了！

绕口令：

/wi ˈgæðəd ˈleðə ənd ˈfeðə fə ðə ˈfjuːtʃə ˈkəuldə ˈweðə/

We gathered leather and feather for the future colder weather.

我们收集了皮革和羽毛以应付将来更冷的天气。

9. /h/

发音要领：嘴唇自然张开，自然呵气，声带不振动。

提示：/h/ 是个清辅音，声音不震动，送气很大，可以拿一张白纸放在嘴前，感受一下气流。不要发成汉语中的"喝"。

绕口令：

/huː meɪd ə həul həul ɪn ðə ˈhəulɪ ˈhəulideɪ)/

Who made a whole hole in the holy holyday?

谁在神圣的假日里打了一个完整的孔？

10. /r/

发音要领：舌尖向上卷起，舌头不要接触任何部位，双唇稍微突出，声带振动。

提示：/r/ 是个浊辅音，声音是由声带震动发出。有些学生会把汉语拼音中的声母 r 的发音来代替 /r/ 的发音，于是把 rose 读成"肉丝"，把 road 读成"肉的"，但实际上两者有很大的差别。

绕口令：

/rɪl rɪˈtɜːnd ðə ˈrɒtn red ˈrædɪʃɪz. ðə ˈrɒtn ˈrædɪʃɪz aː frɒm ˈrɒbət/

Riel returned the rotten red radishes. The rotten radishes are from Robert.

瑞尔把腐烂的红萝卜放回原处。腐烂的萝卜是罗伯特的。

Section C　Announcement Learning

Setting: When the door is closed and the aircraft is about to pushback, the Captain or the Chief flight attendant will make an announcement intended to the flight attendants.

Door Closure Announcement

Ladies and gentlemen, this is Nancy and I'm your chief flight attendant. On behalf of the entire crew, welcome aboard Happy Bird Airlines flight 977F.

Our flight time will be of 7 hours and 30 minutes. We will be flying at an altitude of 6 000 meters at a ground speed of 900 miles per hour.

At this time, make sure your seat backs and tray tables are in their full upright position and that your seat belt is correctly fastened. Also, your portable electronic devices must be set to "airplane" mode until an announcement is made upon arrival. Thank you.

机舱门关闭广播（起飞前广播）

女士们、先生们，我是本次航班的乘务长南茜。我代表全体机组人员，欢迎您乘坐快乐鸟航空公司977F号航班。

我们的飞行时间是7小时30分钟。我们将在6 000米的高度以每小时900英里的地面速度飞行。

此外，在飞机抵达前，您的便携式电子设备必须设置为"飞行"模式。谢谢！

Vocabulary and Expressions

chief /tʃiːf/ *adj.* 首席的，首要的

On behalf of /ɒn bɪˈhɑːf əv/ 代表

entire /ɪnˈtaɪə(r)/ *adj.* 全部的，整个的

altitude /ˈæltɪtjuːd/ *n.* 海拔高度

upright /ˈʌpraɪt/ /ˈrpˈəaɪt/ *adj.* 直立的，垂直的

position /pəˈzɪʃn/ *n.* 位置

seat belt /siːt belt/ 安全带

portable /ˈpɔːtəbl/ *adj.* 便携式的

electronic /ɪˌlekˈtrɒnɪk/ *adj.* 电子的

device /dɪˈvaɪs/ *n.* 设备

fasten /ˈfɑːsn/ *v.* 固定

Check your understanding

1. How long will the fight arrive if the departure time is 9 a.m.?

2. What shall we do with our smartphone?

Tasks

According to sample announcement, make a new announcement by using the prompts given below.

Task 1

Nanning, flight CZ8401, gate 22

Task 2

Changchun, flight CZ6377, gate 30B

Section D　Progress Check

I. Translate the following phrases and words.

1. 安全带

2. 代表

3. 便携式的

4. 电子设备

5. 乘务长

Ⅱ. Translate the following sentences into English.

1. 我代表全体机组人员，欢迎您乘坐快乐鸟航空公司977F号航班。

2. 我们将在6 000米的高度以每小时900英里的地面速度飞行。

3. 在飞机抵达前，您的便携式电子设备必须设置为"飞行"模式。

4. 我们的飞行时间是7小时30分钟。

Ⅲ. Fill in the blanks according to the text.

1. This is Nancy and I'm your_____flight attendant.

2. On behalf of the_____crew, welcome aboard Happybird Airlines flight 977F.

3. Make sure your seat backs and tray tables are in their full_____position and that your seat belt is correctly_____.

4. Our flight time will be_____7 hours and 30 minutes.

Further Reading

Safety Threat

The biggest safety threat facing airlines today may not be a terrorist with a gun, but the man with the portable computer in business class. In the last 15 years, pilots have reported well over 100 incidents that could have been caused by electromagnetic interference. The source of this interference remains unconfirmed, but increasingly, experts are pointing the blame at portable electronic device such as portable computers, radio and cassette players and mobile telephones.

RTCA, an organization which advises the aviation (航空) industry, has recommended that all airlines ban (禁止) such devices from being used during "critical" stages of flight, particularly take-off and landing. Some experts have gone further, calling for a total ban during all flights. Currently, rules on using these devices are left up to individual airlines. And although some airlines prohibit passengers from using such equipment during take-off and landing, most are reluctant to enforce a total ban, given that many passengers want to work during flights.

The difficulty is predicting how electromagnetic fields might affect an aircraft's computers. Experts know that portable device emit radiation which affects those wavelengths which aircraft use for navigation and communication. But, because they have not been able to reproduce these effects in a laboratory, they have no way of knowing whether the interference might be dangerous or not.

The fact that aircraft may be vulnerable (易受损的) to interference raises the risk that terrorists may use radio systems in order to damage navigation equipment. As worrying, though, is the passenger who can't hear the instructions to turn off his radio because the music's too loud.

学习总结

Part II Cabin Service Announcement

Part II Cabin Service Announcement

Module 7 Safety Demonstration

Learning Objective

In this module, you will be able to

1. Read the phonemes of affricate;

2. Use the pronunciation skills of affricate while reading;

3. Read the announcement of safety demonstration;

4. Be dedicated to aviation serving.

视频：安全演示

Guided Learning

Depending on the type of aircraft and presence of a video system, this announcement will be made.

063

Section A Warm-up

I. Answering the following questions.

1. Can you speak out the name of each picture?
2. Do you know something about them?

Fig.7-1   International Airlines

II. Find the definition in Column B which matches the words or phrases in Column A.

A	B
1. Malaysia Airlines	a. 马来西亚航空
2. Lao Airlines	b. 孟加拉航空
3. Bangladesh Airlines	c. 老挝航空
4. Bangkok Airways	d. 曼谷航空

Section B Phonetic Training

破擦音（Affricates）

1. /ts/

发音要领：舌尖先抵住上齿，堵住气流，使气流从舌尖和齿龈间送出，声带不振动。

提示：/ts/ 是个清辅音，声带不震动。/ts/、/dz/、/dr/、/tr/ 是传统的音标符号，新课本中美式、英式读音都没将其包括在内。

绕口令：

/ðə kæts ənd ræts 'sɪtɪŋ ɪn ðə ruːm, ɔːl ðeɪ duː ɪz sɪts ənd ʃɪfts/

The cats and rats sitting in the room, all they do is sits and shifts.

猫和老鼠坐在客厅里，它们所做的就只是坐着、动着。

2．/dz/

发音要领：舌尖先抵住上齿，堵住气流，使气流从舌尖和齿龈间送出。

提示：/dz/ 是个浊辅音，发音时声带震动。/dz/ 有点类似汉语中的"子"（轻音），但发音时有爆破的感觉，而且声带振动较强。

绕口令：

/hiː pʊts hɪz hændz 'ɪntuː ðə bedz tu lʊk fɔː ðə kaː dz ənd kəʊdz/

He puts his hands into the beds to look for the cards and codes.

她把手伸进床里寻找卡片和密码本。

3．/tr/

发音要领：双唇收圆向前突出，舌尖上翘抵住上齿龈，采取发 [r] 的姿势，声带不振动。

提示：/tr/ 是个清辅音，声带不震动。

绕口令：

/'nevə 'trʌbl ə'baʊt 'trʌbl ən'tɪl 'trʌbl 'trʌblz jʊ/

Never trouble about trouble until trouble troubles you!

不要自找麻烦！

4．/dr/

发音要领：双唇收圆向前突出，舌尖上翘抵住上齿龈，采取发 [r] 的姿势，但声带振动。

提示：/dr/ 是个浊辅音，发音时声带震动。有些学生分不清 /dr/ 和 /dʒ/ 的区别，其实发 /dʒ/ 时嘴唇需收圆，同时舌头闭气的部位也比 /dʒ/ 靠前。也有人容易把这个音念成汉语中的"朱"，注意不要在这个音的后面加上元音 /u/。

绕口令：

/ðə 'drʌmə drʌmd ənd hi: dri:md tu bi: ə greɪt 'drʌmə/

The drummer drummed and he dreamed to be a great drummer.

这位鼓手在敲鼓，他梦想成为一名伟大的鼓手。

5．/tʃ/

发音要领：双唇略微张开突出，舌尖抵住上齿龈，用力吐气，声带不振动。

提示：/tʃ/ 是个清辅音，声带不震动。/tʃ/ 这个音和汉语拼音中的声母 ch 很相近，很多北方同学会用"吃"代替 /tʃ/ 是不正确的，一些南方同学会把 /tʃ/ 和汉语拼音中的声母 q 混淆，也是极不正确的，应注意区分它们的异同。

绕口令：

/'tʃerɪ 'ti:tʃɪz 'tʃɪldrən ət tʃɜːtʃ/

Cherry teaches children at church.

彻丽在教堂教孩子们。

6．/dʒ/

发音要领：双唇略微张开突出，舌尖抵住上齿龈，用力吐气，但声带需振动。

提示：/dʒ/ 是个浊辅音，发音时只有微弱气流泻出，摩擦在舌端，声音是由声音震动发出。不要念成汉语中的"基"，"基"字发音舌位靠前，而 /dʒ/ 是用舌尖去顶齿龈，整体舌位不靠前。

绕口令：

/ɪn ðə ɪks'tʃeɪndʒ ðə'ɒrɪndʒɪz a: ə'reɪndʒd 'ɪntu: streɪndʒ 'reɪndʒɪz/

In the exchange the oranges are arranged into strange ranges.

在交易所里橙子被排成奇怪的几排。

Section C Announcement Learning

Setting: The video of demonstration for the use of seat belt and oxygen mask is played for the passengers.

Part II Cabin Service Announcement

Safety Demonstration

Ladies and gentlemen, we will now explain the use of seat belt, oxygen mask and the location of the exit. When the seat belt sign illuminates, you must fasten your seat belt. Insert the metal fittings one into the other and tighten by pulling on the loose end of the strap. To release your seat belt, lift the upper portion of the buckle. We suggest that you keep your seat belt fastened throughout the flight, as we may experience turbulence.

In the event of a decompression, an oxygen mask will automatically appear in front of you. To start the flow of oxygen, pull the mask towards you. Place it firmly over your nose and mouth, secure the elastic band behind your head, and breathe normally. If you are travelling with a child or someone who requires assistance, secure your mask on first, and then assist the other person. Keep your mask on until a uniformed crew member advises you to remove it.

安全演示

女士们、先生们，我们现在将向您说明安全带、氧气面罩的使用和紧急出口的位置。当安全带标志灯亮起时，务必系好安全带。将金属配件一个插入另一个，并通过拉动束带的松动端拧紧。要松开安全带，请提起皮带扣的上部。我们建议您在整个飞行过程中系好安全带，飞行过程中可能会遇到颠簸。

一旦客舱释压，氧气面罩会自动脱落在您面前。氧气的提供需要您把面罩拉向自己，把它牢牢地放在你的鼻子和嘴上，把松紧带固定在头部后面，可以正常呼吸。如果您带着孩子或需要帮助的人旅行，请先戴上面罩，然后再帮助其他人。在没有客舱乘务员协助您的情况下请不要随意将其摘除。

Vocabulary and Expressions

oxygen mask /ˈɒksɪdʒən mɑːsk/ 氧气面罩
location /ləʊˈkeɪʃn/ n. 位置
sign /saɪn/ n. 指示牌
illuminate /ɪˈluːmɪneɪt/ v. 照亮
fasten /ˈfɑːsn/ v. 固定

Insert /ɪn'sɜːt/ v. 插入
metal /'metl/ adj. 金属的
fittings /'fɪtɪŋz/ n. 配件
tighten /'taɪtn/ v. 使变紧，紧固
loose /luːs/ adj. 未固定的，松动的
strap /stræp/ n. 皮带
release /rɪ'liːs/ v. 解开，释放
upper portion /'ʌpər 'pɔːʃn/ 上部
buckle /'bʌkl/ n. 搭扣
turbulence /'tɜːbjələns/ n. 气流
decompression /ˌdiːkəm'preʃn/ n. 减压
automatically /ˌɔːtə'mætɪkli/ adv. 自动地
appear /ə'pɪə(r)/ v. 出现
firmly /'fɜːrmli/ adv. 牢固地
secure /sɪ'kjʊr/ v. 固定
elastic band /ɪ'læstɪk bænd/ 松紧带
breathe /briːð/ v. 呼吸
assistance /ə'sɪstəns/ n. 援助
uniform /'juːnɪfɔːm/ n. 制服
remove /ri'muːv/ v. 摘下

Check your understanding

1. How do you loosen your seat belt?
2. What are the procedures of wearing the oxygen mask?

Tasks

According to sample announcement, make a role-play with your partner.

Task 1

One is flight attendant who is making the announcement, the other one is the passenger fastening his seat belt according to the requirements.

Task 2

One is flight attendant who is making the announcement, the other one is the passenger wearing his oxygen mask according to the requirements.

Section D Progress Check

I. Translate the following phrases and words.

1. 氧气面罩
2. 上部
3. 松紧带
4. 自动地
5. 气流

II. Translate the following sentences into English.

1. 当安全带标志灯亮起时，务必系好安全带。
2. 一旦客舱释压，氧气面罩会自动脱落在您面前。
3. 在没有客舱乘务员协助您的情况下请不要随意将其摘除。
4. 我们建议您在整个飞行过程中系好安全带，飞行过程中可能会遇到颠簸。

III. Fill in the blanks according to the text.

1. We will explain the use of seat belt, oxygen mask and the_____of the exit.

2. We suggest that you keep your seat belt_____throughout the flight, as we may _____turbulence.

3. Place it firmly over your nose and mouth, _____the elastic band behind your head, and_____normally.

4. Insert the_____one into the other and tighten by_____on the loose end of the strap.

Further Reading

Evacuation

On Friday, 7 June, an Italian Airlines flight was ready to leave Rome for Tokyo in Japan. All the passengers were on the plane. The departure time was 21:00. The seatbelt signs were turned on, so passengers were not allowed to stand up and had to stay in their seats. Then something unusual happened.

A woman decided that she had to go to the toilet. So she got up and walked to the back of the plane. The toilet door was clearly marked "TOILET", but the woman opened a door next to the toilet. This door was the emergency exit and, when she opened it, the evacuation slide (逃生滑梯) opened. Because of this, the plane was not able to take off.

All the passengers had to leave the plane. When the evacuation slide has opened, there are two possibilities. Workers can change the slide at the airport, but the flight will be delayed for a long time. Or the plane can take off without an evacuation slide and replace it when it has landed, but the number of passengers on the plane must be smaller for safety reasons.

Thirty-eight passengers had to stay at a hotel at the Airport and take another flight the next day. The other passengers got back on the plane, and it finally took off at 5:10 on Saturday morning. It arrived in Tokyo at 14:10. Some passengers found that their luggage was still in Italy. But perhaps they were lucky...

Part II Cabin Service Announcement

学习总结

Part II Cabin Service Announcement

Module 8　Take-off Announcement

Learning Objective

In this module, you will be able to

1. Understand the meaning of variation of English phonemes;

2. Use the pronunciation skills of variation of English phonemes while reading;

3. Read the announcement of after take-off;

4. Be dedicated to aviation serving.

Guided Learning

Within a minute after take-off, an announcement may be made reminding passengers to keep their seatbelts fastened.

Part Ⅱ Cabin Service Announcement

Section A Warm-up

Ⅰ. Answering the following questions

1. Can you speak out the name of each picture?
2. Do you know something about them?

Fig.8-1 International Airlines

Ⅱ. Find the definition in Column B which matches the word or phrase in Column A.

A	B
1. Thai Airways Internatinal	a. 尼泊尔航空
2. Nepal Airlines	b. 土耳其航空公司
3. Turkish Airlines	c. 日本航空公司
4. Japan Airlines	d. 泰国国际航空公司

Section B Phonetic Training

鼻音、边音和半元音

（Nasals、Lateral Sound and Semi-Vowels）

1. /m/

发音要领：双唇紧闭，舌头平放，气流从鼻腔送出，声带振动。

075

提示：/m/ 是个鼻音、浊辅音，发音时一定是闭拢双唇。发音时会感觉到嘴唇也一起振动。

绕口令：

/aɪ skri:m, jʊ skri:m, wi: ɔ:l skri:m fər 'aɪs kri:m/

I scream, you scream, we all scream for ice-cream!

我叫喊，你叫喊，我们都叫喊着要冰激凌。

2．/n/

发音要领：双唇微开，舌尖抵上齿龈，气流从鼻孔里出来，声带振动。

提示：/n/ 是个鼻音、浊辅音，依靠声带震动发声。/n/ 和 /m/ 是同一组浊辅音，所不同的是 /m/ 是"闭嘴音"，而 /n/ 是"开口音"。

绕口令：

/jʊ nəʊ aɪ nəʊ ðæt jʊ nəʊ. aɪ nəʊ ðæt jʊ nəʊ ðæt aɪ nəʊ/

You know I know that you know. I know that you know that I know.

你知道我知道你知道，我知道你知道我知道。

3．/ŋ/

发音要领：双唇张开，舌尖抵上齿龈，气流从鼻腔送出，声带振动。

提示：/ŋ/ 是个浊辅音，声带震动。很多人会把 /ŋ/ 发成 /n/，/ŋ/ 和汉语拼音中的 ng 音非常相似，它和音标 /n/ 的关系就像汉语拼音中 an-ang，en-eng，in-ing 的关系。

绕口令：

/ðə rɪŋ ɒn ðə sprɪŋ strɪŋ rɪŋz 'djʊərɪŋ 'sprɪŋtaɪm/

The ring on the spring string rings during springtime.

弹簧弦上的环在春天鸣响。

4．/l/

发音要领：舌尖抵住上齿龈，舌尖轻微用力弯曲，气流从舌的旁边送出。

提示：/l/ 是个浊辅音，声音是由声带震动发出。另外要注意清晰音和含糊音两种情况的区别。

绕口令：

/'ju:təlaɪz ðə 'fɜ:təlaɪzə tu ki:p ðə lænd 'fɜ:taɪl/

Utilize the fertilizer to keep the land fertile.

利用化肥保持土地肥沃。

5. /j/

发音要领：嘴形成微笑状，舌尖抵住下齿，舌面贴住上颚，声带振动。

提示：/j/ 是个半元音，发音时口型和元音 /i:/ 有点相似，但它仍是个辅音。元音可以单独成音，可以延长；半元音不可以单独成音，不可以延长。

绕口令：

/ðə 'jeləʊ bɜːd həz jeld fɔː 'menɪ jɪəz ɪn ðə jɑːd əv jeɪl/

The yellow bird has yelled for many years in the yard of Yale.

那只黄色的鸟儿在耶鲁大学的校园里歌唱好多年了。

6. /w/

发音要领：双唇缩小并向前突出，舌后部抬起，嘴慢慢向两边滑开。

提示：/w/ 是个半元音，和元音 /uː/ 很相似。但元音可以单独成音，可以延长；半元音不能单独成音，不可以延长，更不能在它后面附加元音。

绕口令：

/ðə 'wɪti 'wɪtnɪs wɪð'drɔːz hɪz wɜːdz wɪ'ðɪn 'mɪnɪts wɪ'ðaʊt 'enɪ 'riːzn/

The witty witness withdraws his words within minutes without any reason.

机智的证人在几分钟之内毫无理由地收回了他说的话。

Section C Announcement Learning

Setting: It is 10 a.m. The plane has taken off. The attendant will offer the some drinks and meals for the passengers.

Fig.8-2　Attendant

After Take-off Announcement

Ladies and gentlemen, the Captain has turned off the Fasten Seat Belt sign, and you may now move around the cabin. However, we always recommend to keep your seat belt fastened while you're seated.

Flight attendants will be moving through the cabin serving meals and beverages soon. For the convenience of the passenger sitting behind you, please adjust your seat back to its upright and locked position during the meal service. If you need any assistance, please contact any flight attendant. Thank you!

起飞后广播

女士们、先生们，机长已经关闭了"系好安全带"指示灯，现在您可以在客舱内走动了。但是，我们还是建议您在坐好后系好安全带。

稍后，我们将为您提供餐食及各种饮料，希望您能喜欢。在用餐期间，请您调直座椅靠背，以方便后排的旅客。如需要帮助，我们很乐意随时为您服务。谢谢！

Vocabulary and Expressions

turn off /tɜːn əf/ 关掉
cabin /ˈkæbɪn/ n. 机舱
recommend /ˌrekəˈmend/ v. 推荐
serve /sɜːv/ v. 提供
beverage /ˈbevərɪdʒ/ n. 饮料
convenience /kənˈviːnjəns/ n. 方便

adjust /əˈdʒʌst/ v. 调节

upright /ˈʌpraɪt/ adj. 竖直的

lock /lɒk/ v. 锁住

contact /ˈkɒntækt/ v. 联系

Check your understanding

1. How do you do with your seat while you are eating?

2. When can you loosen your seat belt?

Task

Read the sample announcement fluently and precisely.

Section D　Progress Check

I. Translate the following phrases and words.

1. 机舱
2. 调节
3. 关闭
4. 联络
5. 便利

II. Translate the following sentences into English.

1. 稍后，我们将为您提供餐食及各种饮料，希望您能喜欢。
2. 如需要帮助，我们很乐意随时为您服务。
3. 但是，我们还是建议您在坐好后系好安全带。

III. Fill in the blanks according to the text.

1. The Captain has turned off the Fasten Seat Belt sign, and you may now_____the cabin.

2. We always recommend to keep your seat belt fastened_____you're seated.

3. Flight attendants will be moving_____the cabin serving meals and beverages soon.

4. For the convenience of the passenger sitting behind you, please adjust your seat back to its upright and locked position_____the meal service.

Further Reading

Fresh Food, Good Mood

Pick from a choice of **complimentary** dishes on every flight, all **created** with fresh, **seasonal ingredients** and **inspired** by the **destinations** we fly to. Our food is full of flavour and you can enjoy some of your favourite **brands** on board.

On every flight we serve a choice of complimentary meals, snacks and drinks. If it's a short flight, we'll make sure you have time to eat while we're in the air with our quicker express service. And because your safety is always our main **priority**, our **catering facilities** go through **rigorous hygiene testing** before any of our meals are prepared. We've also **streamlined** the **delivery** of our food and drink service in line with strict COVID-19 **guidelines**.

Part II Cabin Service Announcement

学习总结

民航广播词实务
Civil Aviation Broadcasting Practice

Module 9 Descent Announcement

Learning Objective

In this module, you will be able to

1. Understand the meaning of variation of English phonemes;

2. Use the pronunciation skills of variation of English phonemes while reading;

3. Read the announcement of descent;

4. Be dedicated to aviation serving.

Guided Learning

Before, or during the descent, the captain will usually make an announcement with local time and temperature at the destination airport, and time left until arrival.

Part Ⅱ Cabin Service Announcement

Section A Warm-up

I. Answering the following questions.

1. Can you speak out the name of each picture?
2. Do you know something about them?

Fig.9-1 International Airlines

II. Find the definition in Column B which matches the word or phrase in Column A.

A	B
1. Singapore Airlines	a. 印度航空公司
2. Air India	b. 文莱皇家航空公司
3. Vietnam Airlines	c. 新加坡航空公司
4. Royal Brunei Airlines	d. 越南航空

Section B Phonetic Training

音变（Variations）

音变现象包含连读、失去爆破、加音和浊化、变音现象等。

1. 连读（辅音＋元音）

当前一个单词以辅音结尾，后一个单词以元音开头，通常在口语，特别是在快速口语中，它们要连起来读。发音时，前后拼起来。

就像中国的汉语拼音一样。例句：What's the real situation? Let's check it out!（真实情况是什么样的？让我们一起来查看一下。）

2. 失去爆破（辅音＋辅音）

当前一个单词以辅音 p、b、t、d、k、g 结尾，后一个单词又以辅音开头，通常在口语，特别是在快速口语中，它们要连起来读。发音时，前一个辅音保留发音的时候，但不发出来，而后一个辅音则要重读出来。例句：Let me know what you need. I don't know what you say.（让我知道你需要什么。我不知道你说什么。）

3. 加音（元音＋元音）

当前一个单词以元音结尾，后一个单词又以元音开头，通常在口语，特别是在快速口语中，它们要连起来读。发音时，如果前一个元音以 /u/、/au/ 或 /ou/ 结尾，则要在两个元音间加入半元音 /w/；如果前一个元音以 /i/、/ai/、/oi/ 结尾，则要在两个元音间加入半元音 /j/，但不发出来，而后一个辅音则要重读出来。例句：What a coincidence, we meet each other again in the same place!（/w/）（真是太巧了，我们又在同一个地方遇见了。）Don't stop, go on please!（别停下，继续！）（/w/）How are you? I'm going to quit my job!（你好吗？我要辞职了！）

4. 浊化

当一个单词中连续邻近出现两个辅音，后一个辅音要浊化。例句：obody can stop me if I persist!（如果我坚持，没有人能够阻止我。）Your extension number please?（请问你的分机号码是？）He wants to fly in the blue sky!（他想飞翔在蓝天上。）You might as well go to some training school to learn English!（你倒不如去培训学校学英语。）

Fig.9-2　Descent

Section C　Announcement Learning

Setting: It is 10 a.m. The plane is descending. The flight attendant is making an announcement to remind the passengers.

Part Ⅱ　Cabin Service Announcement

Landing Announcement

Good morning, ladies and gentlemen, Our plane is descending now. Please be seated and fasten your seat belt. Seat backs and tables should be returned to the upright position. All personal computers and electronic devices should be turned off. And please make sure that your carry-on items are securely stowed. We will be dimming the cabin lights for landing. Thank you!

飞机下降广播

早上好，女士们、先生们，飞机正在下降。请您回原位坐好，系好安全带，收起小桌板，将座椅靠背调整到正常位置。所有个人电脑及电子设备必须处于关闭状态。请你确认您的手提物品是否已妥善安放。稍后，我们将调暗客舱灯光。谢谢！

Vocabulary and Expressions

descend /dɪ'send/ v. 下降
personal /'pɜːsənl/ adj. 个人的，隐私的
electronic device /ɪˌlek'trɒnɪk dɪ'vaɪs/ 电子设备
carry-on item /'kæriˌɒn 'aɪtəm/ 随身物品
securely /sɪ'kjʊəlɪ/ adv. 安全地
stow /stoʊ/ v. 妥善放置
dim /dɪm/ v. 变暗
land /lænd/ v. 着陆

Check your understanding

1. What is the change for cabin light when the plane is descending?
2. What should we do during the descent?

Task

Read the sample announcement fluently and precisely.

Section D   Progress Check

I. Translate the following phrases and words.

1. 电子设备

2. 随身物品

3. 着陆

4. 下降

5. 妥善放置

II. Translate the following sentences into English.

1. 所有个人电脑及电子设备必须处于关闭状态。
2. 请你确认您的手提物品是否已妥善安放。
3. 稍后，我们将调暗客舱灯光。
4. 将座椅靠背调整到正常位置。

III. Fill in the blanks according to the text.

1. Seat backs and tables should be_____to the upright position.
2. All personal computers and electronic devices should be_____.
3. please make sure that your carry-on items are_____stowed.
4. We will be_____the cabin lights for landing.

Further Reading

Make a Plan

If the plane is going to crash, you almost always have several minutes to prepare before **impact**. Use this time to once again **review** where the exits are, and try to **count** the number of seats between your row and the exit row—that way you'll know when you've reached the exit even if you can't see it.

Assess the situation as well as possible. Try to **determine** what **surface** the plane will land on so you can **customize** your preparations. If you're going to be landing in water, for example, you'll want to put your **life vest** on—don't **inflate** it until you're out of the plane—and if you're going to be landing in cold weather, you should try to get a **blanket** or jacket to keep you warm once outside.

Part Ⅱ Cabin Service Announcement

学习总结

民航广播词实务
Civil Aviation Broadcasting Practice

Module 10 Emergency Landing Announcement

Learning Objective

In this module, you will be able to

1. Understand the meaning of Consonant Blends;

2. Use the pronunciation skills of consonant blends while reading;

3. Read the announcement of emergency landing;

4. Be dedicated to aviation serving.

视频：落地广播

Guided Learning

After touchdown, and as the aircraft is turning off the active runway and taxiing to the gate, the flight attendant will do one last announcement.

Part II　Cabin Service Announcement

Section A　Warm-up

I. Answering the following questions.

1. Can you speak out the name of each picture?
2. Do you know something about them?

Fig.10-1　International Airlines

II. Find the definition in Column B which matches the word or phrase in Column A.

A	B
1. American Airlines	a. 英国航空公司
2. Air Canada	b. 法国航空
3. British Airways	c. 加拿大航空
4. Air France	d. 美国航空

Section B　Phonetic Training

辅音连缀（Consonant Blends）

辅音连缀是指在同一意群内（通常为一个单词内），有两个或两个以上的辅音音素结合在一起的一种语音现象，如 desk /desk/ 中的 /sk/、friend /frend/ 中的 /fr/，以及 spring /spriŋ/ 中的 /spr/ 等。辅音连缀经常发生在词首和词尾。

093

1. 一般读法

在朗读时，任何两个辅音间都不能加上元音，如把 friend/frend/ 读成 /fərend/ 就不对了。正确的方法是第一个音（或第一、第二个音）要读得轻而短，很快过渡到第二个音（或第三个音）上去。

2. /s/ 后面爆破音的读法

当清辅音 /p/ /t/ /k/ 在 /s/ 后面时，无论所属音节重读与否，都不送气，发音类似它们各自相对应的浊辅音，但又不完全相同，区别在于：它们发音时声带不振动。例如：school /sku:l/ n. 学校；student /'stju:d(ə)nt/ n. 学生；spring /sprɪŋ/ n. 春天。

3. 词尾加 -s,-es,-ed 后的读法

（1）一般情况下，可遵循以下规则：清对清，浊对浊，元音也对浊。也就是说词尾音是清辅音，加 -s 或 -ed 之后，就发清辅音 /s/ 或 /t/；词尾音是浊辅音或元音，加了 -s 或 -ed 之后，就发浊辅音 /z/ 或 /d/。例如：books /bʊks/ n. 书籍（复数）；knows /nəʊz/ vt. 知道；asked /æskt/ v. 要求。

（2）词尾音为 /t/、/d/，加 -s 后就分别读成 /ts/ 和 /dz/。例如：cats /kæts/ n. 猫（复数）；gifts /gɪfts/ n. 礼物（复数）；reads /ri:dz/ v. 阅读（第三人称单数）；ends /endz/ v. 结束（第三人称单数）。

（3）词尾音为 /t/、/d/，加 -ed 后，分别读成 /tɪd/ 和 /dɪd/。例如：invited /ɪn'vaɪtɪd/ v. 邀请（过去式）；visited /'vɪzɪtɪd/ v. 拜访（过去式）；needed /'ni:dɪd/ v. 需要（过去式）；pretended /prɪ'tendɪd/ v. 假装（过去式）。

（4）词尾音为 /s/、/z/、/ʃ/、/ʒ/、/tʃ/、/dʒ/ 等，加 -es 后读 /-ɪz/。例如：boxes /'bɒksɪz/ n. 小木箱（复数）；sizes /'saɪzɪz/ n. 大小（复数）；wishes /'wɪʃɪz/ v. 希望（第三人称单数）；watches /wɒtʃɪz/ n. 手表（复数）；bridges /brɪdʒɪz/ n. 桥（复数）。

Section C Announcement Learning

Setting: It is 8 a.m. The plane needs to make an emergency landing, because of a sick passenger on board. The flight attendant is making an announcement to remind the passengers.

Emergency Landing

Ladies and gentlemen, may I have your attention, please. There is a sick passenger on board, and the captain has decided to make an emergency landing at Qingdao airport. We expect to arrive there in 2 hours and 40 minutes. We apologize for any inconvenience. We thank you for your kind support and understanding. Thank you .

紧急迫降广播

女士们、先生们，请大家注意。机上有一名生病的乘客，机长决定在青岛机场紧急迫降。预计2小时40分钟后到达。不便之处，敬请原谅。感谢您的支持和理解。谢谢您！

Vocabulary and Expressions

sick /sɪk/ *adj.* 生病的

emergency landing /ɪˈmɜrdʒənsɪ ˈlændɪŋ/ 紧急迫降

apologize /əˈpɑləˌdʒaɪz/ *v.* 抱歉

support /səˈpɔrt / *v.* 支持

Check your understanding

1. What does the flight need to make an emergency landing?

2. How long will the aircraft arrive at Qingdao airport?

Tasks

According to sample announcement, make a new announcement by using the prompts given below.

Task 1

Zhuhai airport 5 hours 50 minutes

Task 2

Yantai airport 2 hours 10 minutes

Section D   Progress Check

I. Translate the following phrases and words.

1. 紧急迫降

2. 到达

3. 飞机上

4. 不便

5. 抱歉

II. Translate the following sentences into English.

1. 机上有一名生病的乘客，机长决定在青岛机场紧急迫降。

2. 预计 2 小时 40 分钟后到达。

3. 不便之处，敬请原谅。

4. 感谢您的支持和理解。

III. Fill in the blanks according to the text.

Ladies and Gentlemen, May I have your ___1___, please. There is a sick passenger on board, and the captain has ___2___ to make an emergency landing at Qingdao airport. We ___3___ to arrive there in 2 hours and 40 minutes. We apologize ___4___ any inconvenience. We thank you for your kind support and understanding.

Further Reading

Emergency Landing

The airplane from Minneapolis in which Francis Weed was travelling East ran into heavy weather. The sky had been a hazy blue, with the clouds below the plane lying so close together that nothing could be seen of the earth. Then mist began to form outside the windows, and they flew into a white cloud of such density that it reflected the exhaust fires. The color of the cloud darkened to gray, and the plane began to rock.

Francis had been in heavy weather before, but had never been shaken up so much. The man in the seat beside him pulled a flask out of his pocket and took a drink. Francis smiled at his neighbor, but the man looked away; he wasn't sharing his painkiller with anyone.

The plane had begun to drop and flounder wildly. A child was crying. The air in the cabin was overheated and stale, and Francis' left foot went to sleep.

Part II Cabin Service Announcement

He read a little from a paper book that he had bought at the airport, but the violence of the storm divided his attention.

It was black outside the ports. The exhaust fires blazed and shed sparks in the dark, and, inside, the shaded lights, the stuffiness, and the window curtains gave the cabin an atmosphere of intense and misplaced domesticity. Then the lights flickered and went out. "You know what I've always wanted to do?" the man beside Francis said suddenly. "I've always wanted to buy a farm in New Hampshire and raise beef cattle."

The stewardess announced that they were going to make an emergency landing. All but the child saw in their minds the spreading wings of the Angel of Death. The pilot could be heard singing faintly, "I've got sixpence, jolly, jolly sixpence. I've got sixpence to last me all my life…" There was no other sound.

学习总结

Part II Cabin Service Announcement

Attachment 1　Cabin Announcement with Phonetic Symbols

priːˈbɔːdɪŋ əˈnaʊnsmənt
Pre-boarding announcement

gʊd ˈɑːftəˈnuːn ˈpæsɪndʒəz.
Good afternoon passengers.

ðɪs ɪz ðə priːˈbɔːdɪŋ əˈnaʊnsmənt fɔː
This is the pre-boarding announcement for

flaɪt 898 ef tuː ˈpærɪs.
flight 898F to Paris.

wiː ɑː naʊ ɪnˈvaɪtɪŋ ðəʊz ˈpæsɪndʒəz wɪð smɔːl
We are now inviting those passengers with small

ˈtʃɪldrən, ænd ˈeni ˈpæsəndʒərz riˈkwaɪərɪŋ ˈspeʃ(ə)l əˈsɪstəns tu bɪˈɡɪn
children, and any passengers requiring special assistance to begin

ˈbɔːdɪŋ æt ðɪs taɪm. pliz hæv jɔːr ˈbɔːdɪŋ pɑːs ænd aɪˌdentəfɪˈkeɪʃn
boarding at this time. Please have your boarding pass and identification

ˈredɪ. ˈreɡjələr ˈbɔrdɪŋ wɪl bɪˈɡɪn ɪn əˈprɔksəmətli ten ˈmɪnəts taɪm.
ready. Regular boarding will begin in approximately ten minutes time.

θæŋk ju.
Thank you.

101

ˈfaɪnəl ˈbɔːdɪŋ əˈnaʊnsmənt
Final Boarding Announcement

həˈləʊ. ðɪs ɪz ðə ˈfaɪnl ˈbɔːdɪŋ kɔːl fɔː ˈpæsɪndʒəz ˈmɒrɪs ænd ˈlɒri

Hello. This is the final boarding call for passengers Morris and Lorry

bʊkt ɒn flaɪt 778zed tuː ˈhɔŋˈkɒŋ. pliːz prəˈsiːd tuː geɪt 6

booked on flight 778Z to Hongkong. Please proceed to gate 6

ɪˈmiːdiətli. ðə ˈfaɪnl tʃeks ɑː ˈbiːɪŋ kəmˈpliːtɪd ænd ðə ˈkæptɪn wɪl

immediately. The final checks are being completed and the captain will

ˈɔːdə fɔː ðə dɔːz ɒv ðə ˈeəkrɑːft tuː kləʊs ɪn əˈprɒksɪmətli faɪv ˈmɪnɪts. aɪ

order for the doors of the aircraft to close in approximately five minutes. I

rɪˈpiːt. ðɪs ɪz ðə ˈfaɪnl ˈbɔːdɪŋ kɔːl fɔː ˈmɒrɪs ænd ˈlɒri. θæŋk juː.

repeat. This is the final boarding call for Morris and Lorry. Thank you.

Attachment 1　Cabin Announcement with Phonetic Symbols

flaɪt dɪˈleɪ əˈnaʊnsmənt
Flight Delay Announcement

ˈleɪdɪz ænd ˈdʒent(ə)lmən, kæn aɪ hæv jɔːr əˈtɛnʃ(ə)n pliːz?

Ladies and gentlemen, can I have your attention please?

wiː rɪˈgret tuː ɪnˈfɔːm ju ðæt ə ˈθʌndəstɔːm ɪn sɪˈæt(ə)l hæz dɪˈleɪd

We regret to inform you that a thunderstorm in Seattle has delayed

ˈsevrəl flaɪts. flaɪt 797ef tuː ʃæŋˈhaɪ, ˈʃedjuːld fɔː dɪˈpɑːtʃər æt 8:30

several flights. Flight 797F to Shanghai, scheduled for departure at 8:30

frɒm geɪt eɪ, ɪz naʊ ˈʃedjuːld tuː dɪˈpɑːt æt 10:35 frɒm geɪt ef. pliːz

from gate A, is now scheduled to depart at 10:35 from gate F. Please

tʃek ðə əˈraɪvəlz ænd dɪˈpɑːtʃə bɔːdz, ləʊˈkeɪtɪd ɒn ðə ˈkɒŋkɔːsɪz ɒv iːtʃ

check the arrivals and departure boards, located on the concourses of each

meɪn ˈtɜːmɪnl, fɔː mɔː spɪˈsɪfɪk ˌɪnfəˈmeɪʃən ænd ʌpˈdeɪts ɒn ɪndɪˈvɪdjʊəl

main terminal, for more specific information and updates on individual

flaɪts. wiː ɑː ˈsɒri fɔː ði ˌɪnkənˈviːniəns.

flights. We are sorry for the inconvenience.

geɪt ˈtʃeɪndʒɪŋ əˈnaʊnsmənt
Gate Changing Announcement

heˈləʊ. ˈpæsɪndʒəz ɒv flaɪt 571ə baʊnd fɔːr ˈɔːklənd, wɪð stɒps ɪn

Hello. Passengers of flight 571A bound for Auckland, with stops in

Guangzhou, ðə dɪˈpɑːtʃə geɪt hæz biːn tʃeɪndʒd tuː 17dʒiː. ˈɔːlsəʊ, ðeə wɪl

Guanghzou, the departure gate has been changed to 17G. Also, there will

biː ə slaɪt dɪˈpɑːtʃə dɪˈleɪ djuː tuː ɪnˈklɛmənt ˈwɛðər ˌaʊtˈsaɪd. ðiː

be a slight departure delay due to inclement weather outside. The

graʊnd kruː ɪz ɪn ðə ˈprəʊses ɒv deicing ðə wɪŋz ɪn ˌprepəˈreɪʃən fɔː

ground crew is in the process of deicing the wings in preparation for

dɪˈpɑːtʃə. θæŋk juː fɔː jɔː ˈpeɪʃəns.

departure. Thank you for your patience.

Attachment 1 Cabin Announcement with Phonetic Symbols

ˈbɔːdɪŋ əˈnaʊnsmənt
Boarding Announcement

ˈleɪdɪz ænd ˈdʒent(ə)lmən, ðə ˈkæptɪn hæz tɜːnd ɒn ðə ˈfɑːsn siːt

Ladies and gentlemen, the Captain has turned on the Fasten Seat

belt saɪn. ɪf juː hævnt ɔːˈredi dʌn səʊ, pliːz stəʊ jɔː ˈkæri ɒn

Belt sign. If you haven't already done so, please stow your carry-on

ˈlʌgɪdʒ ˌʌndəˈniːθ ðə siːt ɪn frʌnt ɒv juː ɔːr ɪn ən ˈəʊvəhed bɪn. pliːz

luggage underneath the seat in front of you or in an overhead bin. Please

teɪk jɔː siːt ænd ˈfɑːsn jɔː siːt belt. ænd ˈɔːlsəʊ meɪk ʃʊə jɔː siːt

take your seat and fasten your seat belt. And also make sure your seat

bæk ænd ˈfəʊldɪŋ treɪz ɑːr ɪn ðeə fʊl ˈʌpraɪt pəˈzɪʃən.

back and folding trays are in their full upright position.

ɪf juː ɑː ˈsiːtɪd nekst tuː ən ɪˈmɜːdʒənsi ˈeksɪt, pliːz riːd ˈkeəfli ðə

If you are seated next to an emergency exit, please read carefully the

ˈspɛʃəl ɪnˈstrʌkʃənz kɑːd ləʊˈkeɪtɪd baɪ jɔː siːt. ɪf juː duː nɒt wɪʃ tuː

special instructions card located by your seat. If you do not wish to

pəˈfɔːm ðə ˈfʌŋkʃənz dɪsˈkraɪbd ɪn ðə ɪˈvɛnt ɒv ən ɪˈmɜːdʒənsi, pliːz ɑːsk

perform the functions described in the event of an emergency, please ask

ə flaɪt əˈtendənt tuː ˌriːˈsiːt juː.

a flight attendant to reseat you.

wiː ˈrɪmaɪnd juː ðæt ðɪs ɪz ə nɒn-ˈsməʊkɪŋ flaɪt. ˈsməʊkɪŋ ɪz

We remind you that this is a non-smoking flight. Smoking is

prəˈhɪbɪtɪd ɒn ðə ɪnˈtaɪər ˈeəkrɑːft, ɪnˈkluːdɪŋ ðə ˈlævətərɪz. ˈtæmpərɪŋ wɪð,

prohibited on the entire aircraft, including the lavatories. Tampering with,

105

dɪs'eɪblɪŋ ɔː dɪs'trɔɪɪŋ ðə 'lævətəri sməuk dɪ'tektəz ɪz prə'hɪbɪtɪd baɪ lɔː.

disabling or destroying the lavatory smoke detectors is prohibited by law.

Attachment 1 Cabin Announcement with Phonetic Symbols

dɔː 'kləʊʒə
Door Closure

'leɪdɪz ænd 'dʒent (ə) lmən, ðɪs ɪz 'nænsi ænd aɪm jɔː tʃiːf flaɪt
Ladies and gentlemen, this is Nancy and I'm your chief flight

ə'tendənt. ɒn bɪ'hɑːf ɒv ðə ɪn'taɪə kruː, 'welkəm ə'bɔːd hæpi 'bɜːd
attendant. On behalf of the entire crew, welcome aboard Happy Bird

'eəlaɪnz flaɪt 977ef.
Airlines flight 977F.

'aʊə flaɪt taɪm wɪl biː ɒv 7 'aʊəz ænd 30 'mɪnɪts. wiː wɪl biː 'flaɪɪŋ
Our flight time will be of 7 hours and 30 minutes. We will be flying

æt ən 'æltɪtjuːd ɒv 6 000 'miːtəz æt ə graʊnd spiːd ɒv 900 maɪlz pɜːr 'aʊə.
at an altitude of 6 000 meters at a ground speed of 900 miles per hour.

æt ðɪs taɪm, meɪk ʃʊə jɔː siːt bæks ænd treɪ 'teɪblz ɑːr ɪn ðeə fʊl
At this time, make sure your seat backs and tray tables are in their full

'ʌpraɪt pə'zɪʃən ænd ðæt jɔː siːt bɛlt ɪz kə'rektli 'fɑːsnd. 'ɔːlsəʊ, jɔː
upright position and that your seat belt is correctly fastened. Also, your

'pɔːtəbl ɪlɛk'trɒnɪk dɪ'vaɪsɪz mʌst biː set tuː 'eəpleɪn məʊd ən'tɪl æn
portable electronic devices must be set to 'airplane' mode until an

ə'naʊnsmənt ɪz meɪd ə'pɒn ə'raɪvəl. θæŋk juː.
announcement is made upon arrival. Thank you.

107

ˈseɪfti ˌdɛmənsˈtreɪʃən
Safety Demonstration

ˈleɪdɪz ænd ˈdʒent (ə) lmən, wiː wɪl naʊ ɪksˈpleɪn ðə juːz ɒv siːt bɛlt,

Ladies and gentlemen, we will now explain the use of seat belt,

ɒksɪdʒən mɑːsk ænd ðə ləʊˈkeɪʃən ɒv ðə ˈeksɪt. wen ðə siːt belt saɪn

oxygen mask and the location of the exit. When the seat belt sign

ɪˈljuːmɪneɪts, ju mʌst ˈfɑːsn jɔː siːt belt. ˈɪnsət ðə ˈmetl ˈfɪtɪŋz wʌn

illuminates, you must fasten your seat belt. Insert the metal fittings one

ˈɪntuː ðə ˈʌðər ænd ˈtaɪtn baɪ ˈpʊlɪŋ ɒn ðə luːs end ɒv ðə stræp. tuː

into the other and tighten by pulling on the loose end of the strap. To

rɪˈliːs jɔː siːt belt, lɪft ðə ˈʌpə ˈpɔːʃən ɒv ðə ˈbʌkl. wiː səˈdʒest ðæt

release your seat belt, lift the upper portion of the buckle. We suggest that

ju kiːp jɔː siːt belt ˈfɑːsnd θruː(ː)ˈaʊt ðə flaɪt, æz wiː meɪ

you keep your seat belt fastened throughout the flight, as we may

ɪksˈpɪərɪəns ˈtɜːbjələns.

experience turbulence.

ɪn ðə ɪˈvent ɒv ə diːkəmˈpreʃ(ə)n, æn ˈɒksɪdʒən mɑːsk wɪl ɔːtəˈmætɪkəl

In the event of a decompression, an oxygen mask will automatically

əˈpɪər ɪn frʌnt ɒv ju. tuː stɑːt ðə fləʊ ɒv ˈɒksɪdʒən, pʊl ðə mɑːsk təˈwɔːdz

appear in front of you. To start the flow of oxygen, pull the mask towards

ju. pleɪs ɪt ˈfɜːmli ˈəʊvə jɔː nəʊz ænd maʊθ, sɪˈkjʊə ðə ɪˈlæstɪk bænd

you. Place it firmly over your nose and mouth, secure the elastic band

bɪˈhaɪnd jɔː hed, ænd briːð ˈnɔːməli. ɪf ju ɑː ˈtrævlɪŋ wɪð ə tʃaɪld

behind your head, and breathe normally. If you are travelling with a child

Attachment 1 Cabin Announcement with Phonetic Symbols

ɔː 'sʌmwʌn huː rɪ'kwaɪəz ə'sɪstəns, sɪ'kjuə jɔː maːsk ɒn fɜːst, ænd ðen

or someone who requires assistance, secure your mask on first, and then

ə'sɪst ðə 'ʌðə 'pɜːsn. kiːp jɔː maːsk ɒn ən'tɪl ə 'juːnɪfɔːmd kruː

assist the other person. Keep your mask on until a uniformed crew

'membər əd'vaɪzɪz ju tuː rɪ'muːv ɪt.

member advises you to remove it.

109

'ɑːftə 'teɪkɒf
After Take-off

'leɪdɪz ænd 'dʒent(ə)lmən, ðə 'kæptɪn hæz tɜːnd ɒf ðə 'fɑːsn siːt

Ladies and gentlemen, the Captain has turned off the Fasten Seat

belt saɪn, ænd ju meɪ naʊ muːv ə'raʊnd ðə 'kæbɪn. haʊ'evə, wiː 'ɔːlweɪz

Belt sign, and you may now move around the cabin. However, we always

ˌrekə'mɛnd tuː kiːp jɔː siːt belt 'fɑːsnd waɪl jʊə 'siːtɪd

recommend to keep your seat belt fastened while you' re seated.

flaɪt ə'tendənts wɪl biː 'muːvɪŋ θruː ðə 'kæbɪn 'sɜːvɪŋ miːlz

Flight attendants will be moving through the cabin serving meals

ænd 'bevərɪdʒɪz suːn. fɔː ðə kən'viːniəns ɒv ðə 'pæsɪndʒə 'sɪtɪŋ bɪ'haɪnd

and beverages soon. For the convenience of the passenger sitting behind

ju, pliːz ə'dʒʌst jɔː siːt bæk tuː ɪts 'ʌpraɪt ænd lɒkt pə'zɪʃən 'djʊərɪŋ

you, please adjust your seat back to its upright and locked position during

ðə miːl 'sɜːvɪs. ɪf ju niːd 'eni ə'sɪstəns, pliːz 'kɒntækt 'eni flaɪt

the meal service. If you need any assistance, please contact any flight

ə'tendənt. θæŋk ju.

attendant. Thank you.

Attachment 1 Cabin Announcement with Phonetic Symbols

dɪˈsent
Descent

gʊd ˈmɔːnɪŋ, ˈleɪdɪz ænd ˈdʒent(ə)lmən, ˈaʊə pleɪn ɪz dɪˈsendɪŋ naʊ.

Good morning, ladies and gentlemen, Our plane is descending now.

pliːz biː ˈsiːtɪd ænd ˈfɑːsn jɔː siːt belt. siːt bæks ænd ˈteɪblz ʃʊd biː

Please be seated and fasten your seat belt. Seat backs and tables should be

rɪˈtɜːnd tuː ðə ˈʌpraɪt pəˈzɪʃən. ɔːl ˈpɜːsnl kəmˈpjuːtəz ænd ɪlekˈtrɒnɪk

returned to the upright position. All personal computers and electronic

dɪˈvaɪsɪz ʃʊd biː tɜːnd ɒf. ænd pliːz meɪk ʃʊə ðæt jɔː ˈkæri ɒn

devices should be turned off. And please make sure that your carry-on

ˈaɪtəmz ɑː sɪˈkjʊəli stəʊd. wiː wɪl biː ˈdɪmɪŋ ðə ˈkæbɪn laɪts fɔː

items are securely stowed. We will be dimming the cabin lights for

ˈlændɪŋ. θæŋk ju!

landing. Thank you!

111

ɪˈmɜːdʒənsi ˈlændɪŋ
Emergency Landing

ˈleɪdɪz ænd ˈdʒent(ə)lmən, meɪ aɪ hæv jɔːr əˈtenʃ(ə)n, pliːz. ðeər ɪz eɪ

Ladies and Gentlemen, May I have your attention, please. There is a

sɪk ˈpæsɪndʒər ɒn bɔːd, ænd ðə ˈkæptɪn hæz dɪˈsaɪdɪd tuː meɪk ə

sick passenger on board, and the captain has decided to make an

ɪˈmɜːdʒənsi ˈlændɪŋ æt Qingdao ˈeəpɔːt. wiː ɪksˈpekt tuː əˈraɪv ðeər ɪn 2

emergency landing at Qingdao airport. We expect to arrive there in 2

ˈaʊəz ænd 40 ˈmɪnɪts. wiː əˈpɒlədʒaɪz fɔːrˈeni ɪnkənˈviːniəns. wiː θæŋk ju

hours and 40 minutes. We apologize for any inconvenience. We thank you

fɔː jɔː kaɪnd səˈpɔːt ænd ˌʌndəˈstændɪŋ. θæŋk ju.

for your kind support and understanding. Thank you.

Attachment 2　The World Leading Airlines

阿勒马克图姆国际机场
Al Maktoum International Airport

【简介】

阿勒马克图姆国际机场（Al Maktoum International Airport）是在阿拉伯联合酋长国迪拜杰贝阿里的一个主要机场的正式名称，2010年6月27日竣工，是迪拜世界中心的一部分。以前有过的名称包括"杰贝阿里国际机场""杰贝阿里机场城"和"迪拜世界中心国际机场"。它的名字是为了纪念已故酋长迪拜前国王马克图姆·本·拉希德·阿勒马克图姆。

它开通时只有一条跑道，而且只起降货运航班。

【标志】

【知识加油站】

机场名称	阿勒马克图姆国际机场 Al Maktoum International Airport
IATA	DWC
ICAO	OMDW
国家地区	阿联酋
所在地区	迪拜

奥黑尔国际机场
O'Hare International Airport

【简介】

奥黑尔国际机场（O'Hare International Airport）是美国伊利诺伊州芝加哥市的主要机场，位于市中心西北 27 千米。自 1960 年代扩建完成直到 1998 年，奥黑尔国际机场一直是世界上客流量最大的机场。1998 年后，亚特兰大哈兹菲尔德－杰克逊国际机场在客运流量上超过奥黑尔国际机场。目前，奥黑尔国际机场仍是世界上起降次数最多的机场。奥黑尔国际机场是美国第四大国际航空枢纽，排在肯尼迪国际机场、洛杉矶国际机场和迈阿密国际机场之后。奥黑尔国际机场是美国联合航空的第二大基地和中转枢纽，也是美国航空的第二大枢纽。奥黑尔国际机场共有 8 条跑道，其中最长的约 4 140 米。此外另有 3 条跑道的长度也达到约 2 743 米，足够大型客机起降。

【标志】

Chicago O'Hare International AIRPORT

【知识加油站】

机场名称	奥黑尔国际机场 O'Hare International Airport
IATA	ORD
ICAO	KORD
国家地区	美国
所在地区	芝加哥市

北京大兴国际机场
Beijing Daxing International Airport

【简介】

北京大兴国际机场（Beijing Daxing International Airport），位于中国北京市大兴区榆垡镇、礼贤镇和河北省廊坊市广阳区之间，北距天安门46千米、北京首都国际机场67千米，南距雄安新区55千米，西距北京南郊机场约640米（围场距离），为4F级国际机场、世界级航空枢纽、国家发展新动力源。

2014年12月26日，北京新机场项目开工建设；2018年9月14日，北京新机场项目定名"北京大兴国际机场"；2019年9月25日，北京大兴国际机场正式通航，北京南苑机场正式关闭；2019年10月27日，北京大兴国际机场航空口岸正式对外开放。

【标志】

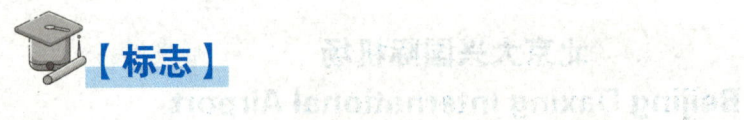

daxing
PKX airport

【知识加油站】

机场名称	北京大兴国际机场 Beijing Daxing International Airport
IATA	PKX
ICAO	ZBAD
国家地区	中国
飞行区等级	4F
地区管理	中国民用航空华北地区管理局

伦敦希思罗机场
London Heathrow Airport

【简介】

伦敦希思罗机场（London Heathrow Airport），通常简称为希思罗机场，位于英国英格兰大伦敦希灵登区，东距伦敦中心有 23 千米。此机场拥有 2 条平行的东西向跑道及 4 座航站楼，为伦敦最主要的国际机场，也是全英国乃至全世界最繁忙的机场之一。2014 年总客运量在全球众多机场中排行第 3，次于美国的亚特兰大机场和中国的北京首都国际机场。由于机场开出众多的跨境航班，因此以跨境的客量计算，希思罗机场的客流量是最高的。同时，希思罗机场是全欧洲最繁忙的机场，比巴黎戴高乐机场及法兰克福国际机场的客流量还要高出 31.5%，但航班数目则比该两个机场的总和少 1/3。这反映出由于航班数目限制下，航空公司多利用载客量高的广体式客机（如空中客车 A380、波音 747、波音 777）营运来往希思罗机场的航线。

【标志】

Heathrow

【知识加油站】

机场名称	伦敦希思罗机场 London Heathrow Airport
IATA	LHR
ICAO	EGLL
国家地区	英国
飞行区等级	4F
地区管理	英国民用航空管理局

约翰·菲茨杰拉德·肯尼迪国际机场
John Fitzgerald. Kennedy International Airport

【简介】

约翰·菲茨杰拉德·肯尼迪国际机场又称为约翰·F.肯尼迪国际机场（John F. Kennedy International Airport），简称为"肯尼迪国际机场"或"爱德怀德机场"，位于纽约皇后区（昆斯区）牙买加湾之滨，是纽约市的主要国际机场，距离曼哈顿下城19千米，也是全世界最大机场之一。该机场由纽约与新泽西港口事务管理局运营（该管理局同时还管理拉瓜地亚机场、纽瓦克自由国际机场等大纽约都会区的机场）。该机场内有超过90间航空公司营运。肯尼迪国际机场是捷蓝航空的枢纽机场，也是美国航空和达美航空主要国际航班的枢纽机场。肯尼迪国际机场是美国航空第四个枢纽机场和达美航空第五个枢纽机场。过去，这个机场是美国东方航空、国家航空、泛美航空和环球航空的枢纽机场。跑道13R-31L是北美地区第二长的商用跑道。

【标志】

T4 | JFK INTERNATIONAL AIR TERMINAL

【知识加油站】

机场名称	约翰·菲茨杰拉德·肯尼迪国际机场 John F. Kennedy International Airport
IATA	JFK
ICAO	KJFK
国家地区	美国
飞行区等级	4F
地区管理	美国联邦航空局

洛杉矶国际机场
Los Angeles International Airport

【简介】

洛杉矶国际机场（Los Angeles International Airport）是美国加州大洛杉矶地区的主要机场，位于美国加利福尼亚州，距洛杉矶市中心19千米，紧邻太平洋，为美国门户型国际机场。1941年更名为"洛杉矶机场"；1947年，洛杉矶机场启用"LAX"为其代码；1947年，更名为洛杉矶国际机场。

就搭乘直达班机的旅客数量而言（非衔接航班），在全球众多机场之中，洛杉矶国际机场名列前茅。

因为该机场位于太平洋岸边，浓雾有时影响班机起降，此时，部分航班会选择就近转降47英里（76千米）外圣博那蒂诺县（San Bernardino）的安大略国际机场。

【标志】

【知识加油站】

机场名称	洛杉矶国际机场 Los Angeles International Airport
IATA	LAX
ICAO	KLAX
国家地区	美国
飞行区等级	4F
运营机构	洛杉矶世界机场

上海浦东国际机场
Shanghai Pudong International Airport

【简介】

上海浦东国际机场（Shanghai Pudong International Airport），位于中国上海市浦东新区，距上海市中心约 30 千米、上海虹桥机场约 40 千米。现由上海机场（集团）有限公司进行经营管理工作。

2012 年，上海浦东国际机场客运量位列中国大陆第三，同时也是货邮运量大陆第一，世界第三的机场。2019 年，上海浦东国际机场共保障飞机起降 511 846 架次，完成旅客吞吐量 7 615.34 万人次，货邮吞吐量 363.56 万吨。

【标志】

【知识加油站】

机场名称	上海浦东国际机场 Shanghai Pudong International Airport
IATA	PVG
ICAO	ZSPD
国家地区	中国
飞行区等级	4F
地区管理	中国民用航空华东地区管理

成田国际机场
Narita International Airport

【简介】

成田国际机场（Narita International Airport）又称"东京成田国际机场"，位于日本千叶县成田市，西距东京都中心 63.5 千米，是日本最大的国际机场，也是东京主要的联外国际机场，年客流量居日本第二位，货运吞吐量居日本第一。据 2020 年 7 月成田国际机场株式会社官网显示，成田国际机场共有 3 座航站大楼、2 条跑道。为了与东京另一座联外机场东京国际机场（羽田机场）区别，国际上常以"东京成田机场"（Tokyo-Narita）称呼，有时也会直接以"东京机场"称呼。1978 年启用后，来往东京的国际航班主要在此起降，羽田机场则转以负责国内航线为主。

【标志】

【知识加油站】

机场名称	成田国际机场 Narita International Airport
IATA	NRT
ICAO	RJAA
国家地区	日本
飞行区等级	4F
地区管理	日本国土交通省东京航空局

巴黎夏尔·戴高乐机场
Pairs Charles de Gaulle Airport

【简介】

巴黎夏尔·戴高乐机场（法语：Aéroport Paris Charles de Gaulle），简称"戴高乐机场"，是法国首都巴黎首要的机场，为欧洲主要的航空中心之一，也是法国主要的国际机场。它是以法兰西第五共和国第一任总统夏尔·戴高乐的名字命名的。

其位于离巴黎市中心东北 25 千米处的鲁瓦西（隶属法兰西岛大区的瓦勒德瓦兹省），也因此被称为鲁瓦西机场（Roissy），占地面积为 32.38 平方千米（32.57 公顷）。据 2020 年 6 月机场官网显示，巴黎夏尔·戴高乐机场有 3 座客运主航站楼、6 座航空贸站、4 条跑道。

【标志】

AÉROPORTS DE PARIS

【知识加油站】

机场名称	巴黎夏尔·戴高乐机场 Pairs Charles de Gaulle Airport
IATA	CDG
ICAO	LFPG
国家地区	法国
飞行区等级	4F
地区管理	法国民航总局

香港国际机场
Hong Kong International Airport

【简介】

　　香港国际机场（Hong Kong International Airport，HKIA），也称香港赤鱲角国际机场（Chek Lap Kok Airport），是香港现时唯一的民航机场，位于新界大屿山赤鱲角（chi lie jiao），占地面积为 12.55 平方千米，设有三条跑道，由香港机场管理局管理，也是全世界最繁忙的机场之一。香港国际机场为国泰航空、华民航空、香港航空及香港快运航空的枢纽机场，同时为寰宇一家的其中一个枢纽机场。香港国际机场被英国独立航空调查机构（Skytrax）评为五星级机场，于 2001 年至 2012 年一直跻身三甲，期间八次被评为"全球最佳机场"。此外，香港国际机场于 2006 年至 2008 年及 2010 年 4 次被知名商务旅游杂志《商旅》评为中国最佳机场，于 2012 年的《旅游行业报》旅游大奖选举中，连续 10 届获选为最佳，并且在年客运量逾 4 000 万人次的机场类别中，被国际机场协会推选为全球最佳。

【标志】

【知识加油站】

机场名称	香港国际机场 Hong Kong International Airport
IATA	HKG
ICAO	VHHH
国家地区	中国
时区	UTC+08:00
地区管理	香港机场管理局

Attachment 3 The World Leading Airports

卡塔尔航空
Qatar Airways

【简介】

卡塔尔航空（Qatar Airways），是一家总部设于卡塔尔首都多哈的国际航空公司，是寰宇一家及阿拉伯航空协会成员之一。它以哈马德国际机场为主要基地，至今已开通了全球150多个国际城市的航线。

卡塔尔航空于1993年11月22日成立，并于1994年1月20日起正式开始商业飞行。成立初期，公司由卡塔尔部分王室成员控股。1997年4月，由一个新的管理团队获得公司管理权。现在，卡塔尔航空由卡塔尔政府和个人投资者各占50%股份。

卡塔尔航空优惠俱乐部的飞行常客计划有着全世界最高的获奖

率，同时卡塔尔航空也是全世界 7 家 Skytrax 五星级航空公司之一。2013 年 10 月 30 日卡塔尔航空正式加盟寰宇一家。

【标志】

【知识加油站】

航空公司	卡塔尔航空 Qatar Airways
IATA	QR
ICAO	QTR
联盟	寰宇一家

新西兰航空
Air New Zealand

【简介】

新西兰航空（Air New Zealand，AIZ）是新西兰最大的航空公司，是一家经营国际和新西兰国内航空业务的集团公司，提供新西兰国内和往返澳大利亚、西南太平洋、亚洲、北美和英国等国际航线的旅客和货物航空运输的服务。其最大的航空基地设在奥克兰。它是星空联盟的成员之一。航空公司下属有一个名为新西兰支线航空的品牌，当中包括尼尔逊航空、飞鹰航空和库克山航空。

【标志】

【知识加油站】

航空公司	新西兰航空 Air New Zealand
IATA	NZ
ICAO	ANZ
联盟	星空联盟
网站	http://www.airnewzealand.co.nz

新加坡航空
Singapore Airlines

【简介】

新加坡航空有限公司（简称新航，英语：Singapore Airlines，马来语：Syarikat Penerbangan）是新加坡的国家航空公司。新加坡航空以樟宜机场为基地，主要经营国际航线，在东南亚、东亚和南亚拥有强大的航线网络，并占据袋鼠航线的一部分市场。除此之外，新加坡航空的业务还有跨太平洋航班，包括以 A340-500 营运的直航航班新加坡－纽约和新加坡－洛杉矶。新航还是首个营运全球最大型的客机 A380 的航空公司。

新加坡航空在《财星》杂志 2007 年全球最被受欣赏的公司中排行第 17 位，航空公司当中排行第 2 位，其品牌在航空界中已广为人知，尤其是在安全、服务素质和革新风格方面，与其收益成比例。新航获奖无数，对机队购买颇为乐观，勇于尝试不同新机种。新航亦是亚洲首家、全球第三家被通过为 IOSA（运行安全审计）。在客舱服务排名方面，新航为亚洲第二（亚洲第一为马来西亚航空）。

【标志】

SINGAPORE AIRLINES

【知识加油站】

航空公司	新加坡航空 Singapore Airlines
IATA	SQ
ICAO	SIA
联盟	星空联盟
网站	https://www.singaporeair.com/

澳洲航空公司
Qantas Airway

【简介】

澳洲航空公司(Qantas Airways)简称澳航，也称为"飞行袋鼠"(The Flying Kangaroo)，是澳洲最大的航空公司，也是全球第三历史悠久的航空公司，仅次于荷兰皇家航空和哥伦比亚航空。其总部设于悉尼，以悉尼和墨尔本机场为主要枢纽机场。澳洲航空自1951年以来从未发生死亡事故，因此被认为是世界上安全纪录最好的大型航空公司之一。

【标志】

Attachment 3　The World Leading Airports

【知识加油站】

航空公司	澳洲航空公司 Qantas Airways
IATA	QF
ICAO	QFA
联盟	寰宇一家
网站	https://www.qantas.com.au/

阿联酋航空公司
Emirates Airline

【简介】

阿联酋航空公司（Emirates Airline），又称阿拉伯联合酋长国航空公司，成立于 1985 年 10 月 25 日，其向政府贷款 1 000 万美元启动公司业务，当时只有 2 架租来的飞机和 3 条航线，成立短短 5 个月后，阿联酋航空就将自己的第一架飞机送上了蓝天，总部设于迪拜，以迪拜国际机场为基地，阿联酋航空公司的母公司称为阿联酋航空集团（The Emirates Group）。阿联酋航空由迪拜酋长国政府拥有。

阿联酋航空是全球发展最快的航空公司之一，是世界为数不多的清一色大型飞机的航空公司。阿联酋航空订购的空客 A380 飞机总数达到 140 架，截止至 2017 年 1 月，已接收 93 架空客 A380 飞机。

【标志】

Emirates

【知识加油站】

航空公司	阿联酋航空公司 Emirates Airline
IATA	EK
ICAO	UAE
网站	https://www.emirates.com/

中国国际航空
Air China

【简介】

中国国际航空股份有限公司（Air China），简称"国航"，是中国最大的国有航空企业，也是中国唯一载国旗飞行的民用航空公司。其总部设在北京，以北京首都国际机场为基地。其前身中国国际航空公司成立于1988年。2002年10月，中国国际航空公司联合中国航空总公司和中国西南航空公司，成立了中国航空集团公司，并以联合三方的航空运输资源为基础，组建新的中国国际航空公司。中国航空集团公司与中国东方航空集团公司和中国南方航空集团公司合称中国三大航空集团，经营业务包括航空客运、航空货运及物流三大核心产业。

【标志】

AIR CHINA 中国国际航空公司

【知识加油站】

航空公司	中国国际航空 Air China
IATA	CA
ICAO	CCA
联盟	星空联盟
网站	http://www.airchina.com.cn/

中国南方航空
China Southern Airlines

【简介】

中国南方航空集团有限公司是一家总部设在广州的中央企业，与中国航空集团公司和中国东方航空集团公司合称中国三大航空集团。中国南方航空集团有限公司（China Southern Airlines），简称"南航"，以蓝色垂直尾翼镶红色木棉花为公司标志，主要提供航空客运、货运及邮运服务。在 2013 年，南航的旅客运输量达 9 180 万人次，货邮运输量 128 万吨，运输总周转量 175 亿吨千米，分别占中国民航总量的 30.2%、20.5%、24.4%。以载客总量计，2010 年南航以全年运输旅客 8 000 万人次位居世界第三，仅次于美国航空及达美航空，为当年全亚洲载客量及飞机数量最多的航空公司。南航亦是天合联盟成员，在亚洲区将主要与大韩航空及达美航空进行全面的代码共享的协议。2011 年 10 月 14 日，空中客车公司向南航交付首架空客 A380 客机，使得南航成为中国首家、全球第七家营运空中客车 A380 飞机的航空公司和全球第一家同时营运 A380 与波音 787 的航空公司。

【标志】

中国南方航空
CHINA SOUTHERN

【知识加油站】

航空公司	中国南方航空 China Southern Airlines
IATA	CZ
ICAO	CSN
联盟	天合联盟
网站	https://www.csairgroup.cn/

中国东方航空
China Eastern Airlines

【简介】

中国东方航空集团有限公司，简称"东航"（China Eastern），是一家总部设在中国上海的国有控股航空公司，为中国三大航空公司之一。其设有飞行常客计划"东方万里行"，1997年成为首家在纽约、香港、上海三地上市的中国航企。在原中国东方航空集团公司的基础上，兼并中国西北航空公司，联合中国云南航空公司所组成的新集团，与中国航空集团公司和中国南方航空集团公司合称中国三大航空集团，并在2010年完成了与上海航空公司的联合重组。除主要的航空运输业务外，东航还运营航空食品、进出口、传媒广告、旅游票务、机场投资等其他次要业务。

【标志】

中國東方航空
CHINA EASTERN

【知识加油站】

航空公司	中国东方航空 China Eastern Airlines
IATA	MU
ICAO	CES
联盟	天合联盟
网站	http://www.ceair.com/

国泰航空公司
Cathay Pacific Airways Limited

【简介】

国泰航空有限公司简称国泰航空公司（Cathay Pacific Airways Limited），是香港第一所提供民航服务的航空公司，为太古集团及寰宇一家成员，以香港国际机场作为枢纽。国泰航空公司的主要业务是经营定期航空业务、航空货运、航空饮食及航机处理。

国泰航空公司是目前全球唯一一家，4次赢得世界航空业权威机构Skytrax的"年度最佳航空公司"大奖的航空公司（2003，2005，2009及2014年），在世界航空业界拥有良好声誉。国泰航空公司也是Skytrax五星级航空公司之一。

【标志】

Attachment 3　The World Leading Airports

【知识加油站】

航空公司	国泰航空公司 Cathay Pacific Airways Limited
IATA	CX
ICAO	CPA
联盟	寰宇一家
网站	https://www.cathaypacific.com/

维珍大西洋航空公司
Virgin Atlantic Airways

【简介】

维珍航空是英国维珍大西洋航空公司（Virgin Atlantic Airways）的简称。维珍航空于 1984 年成立，是英国一家航空公司，提供来往英国的洲际长途航空服务。维珍航空是维珍集团的附属公司之一，维珍集团拥有其 51% 股权，达美航空则拥有 49% 股权。

【标志】

【知识加油站】

航空公司	维珍大西洋航空公司 Virgin Atlantic Airways
IATA	VS
ICAO	VIR
网站	http://www.virgin-atlantic.com/

美国联合航空公司
United Airlines

【简介】

美国联合航空公司（United Airlines）是美国一家大型航空公司，简称"联航"，在中国大陆则被简称为"美联航"，以与中国联合航空（中联航）区别。其总部位于美国伊利诺伊州芝加哥市郊，邻近其主要枢纽机场芝加哥奥黑尔国际机场。至2011年7月31日为止，以总乘客量计算，其为世界第二大航空公司，仅次于美国航空之后；以总乘客飞行里程数计算，则是世界第三大航空公司，居于美国航空及达美航空之后。美国联合航空公司也是星空联盟的创始成员之一。

联航曾于2002年12月9日向美国政府申请美国法令第11章破产保护，并于2006年2月1日脱离破产保护，这是历史上最大以及历时最长的航空公司破产保护案件。2011年11月30日，联航与美国大陆航空达成合并协议，双方的合并程序逐步进行，两家公司先后在均有业务的机场进行航站柜台、登机位等地勤服务的搬迁整合和标志更换。同时，联航"红地毯贵宾室"（Red Carpet Club）与"大陆航空贵宾室"（Presidents Club）合并成为"联合航空贵宾室"（United Club）。2012年3月3日，大陆的飞行常客奖励计划"翼通天下"（OnePass）并入联合"前程万里"（MileagePlus）计划，大陆航空品牌也在同日起正式消失。

【标志】

UNITED

【知识加油站】

航空公司	美国联合航空公司 United Airlines
IATA	UA
ICAO	UAL
联盟	星空联盟
网站	https://www.united.com/zh-hans/cn/

英国航空公司
British Airways

【简介】

英国航空公司（British Airways）简称"英航"，是英国的国家航空公司，也是英国历史最悠久的航空公司，为寰宇一家的创始会员之一。其主要枢纽是伦敦希思罗机场及伦敦格域机场。英航是全球最大的国际航空客运公司之一，全球第七大之货运航空公司，欧洲第二大航空公司，西欧最大的航空公司之一，全球两间曾拥有协和客机的航空公司之一，另一间曾拥有协和客机的航空公司为法国航空。

【标志】

Attachment 3　The World Leading Airports

【知识加油站】

航空公司	英国航空公司 British Airways
IATA	BA
ICAO	BAW
联盟	寰宇一家
网站	https://www.britishairways.com/travel/home/public/zh_cn

汉莎航空
Deutsche Lufthansa（德语）

【简介】

德国汉莎航空股份公司（德语：Deutsche Lufthansa AG），简称"汉莎航空"，又称为"德航"，是德国的国家航空公司。按照载客量和机队规模计算，为欧洲最大的航空公司；按照乘客载运量计算，为世界第四大航空公司。其德文，原意是"空中的汉莎"，而名称中的"汉莎"源自13—15世纪北德地区强大的商业联盟汉萨同盟。

汉莎航空的总部设于北威州科隆，枢纽机场则为法兰克福机场，其客运和货运服务的经营中心位于法兰克福。德国政府在1997年以前持有汉莎航空35.68%的股份，目前则由私人投资者控股（88.52%）。汉莎航空在1997年成为星空联盟的创始成员。目前在146个国家有117 000名员工。2010年汉莎航空承载旅客量超过9 000万。

Attachment 3　The World Leading Airports

【标志】

Lufthansa

【知识加油站】

航空公司	汉莎航空 Deutsche Lufthansa（德语）
IATA 代码	LH
ICAO 代码	DLH
联盟	星空联盟
网站	https://www.lufthansa.com/cn/zh

全日空航空公司
All Nippon Airways

【简介】

全日空航空公司简称"全日空",是日本的航空公司,成立于1952年12月27日,为星空联盟成员,总部位于东京汐留。原为日本营运规模第二大的航空公司,但于2010年1月日本航空破产后取而代之,成为日本第一大航空公司。

它的主要国内枢纽是在东京国际机场(羽田)、大阪国际机场(伊丹)、中部国际机场(近名古屋)及新千岁机场(靠近札幌)。

【标志】

【知识加油站】

航空公司	全日空航空公司 All Nippon Airways
IATA 代码	NH
ICAO 代码	ANA
联盟	星空联盟
网站	https://www.ana.co.jp/en/us/

芬兰航空公司
Finn Air

【简介】

芬兰航空公司（Finn Air）是芬兰最大的航空公司和国家航空公司（Flag Carrier），以赫尔辛基－万塔机场作为枢纽。它和其子公司支配着芬兰国内和国际航空运输市场。它也是航空联盟寰宇一家的成员之一。2006 年，其客量为 880 万。它的航线网络覆盖了 20 个国内城市和 50 的个国际城市，另外还营运一些包机航班。它也是历史最悠久的航空公司之一。2018 年 5 月，芬兰航空公司在"世界十大最安全航空公司"中名列第三位。

【标志】

FINNAIR

【知识加油站】

航空公司	芬兰航空公司 Finn Air
IATA 代码	AY
ICAO 代码	FIN
联盟	寰宇一家
网站	https://www.finnair.com

References

[1] 高峰. 空乘情景英语教程［M］. 北京：中国民航出版社，2018.

[2] 李勇. 乘务员英语水平考试指南［M］. 北京：中国民航出版社，2009.

[3] 刘玉梅. 民航乘务员培训教程［M］. 北京：中国民航出版社，2007.

[4] 朱林莉，高玉清. 民航情景英语［M］. 北京：中国人民大学出版社，2020.

[5] 李永. 民航乘务员基础教程［M］. 北京：中国民航出版社，2011.

[6] 中国民航网 http://www.caacnews.com.cn/.

[7] 民航资源网 http://www.carnoc.com/.

[8] 首都机场集团有限公司 http://www.cah.com.cn/index.jspx.

[9] 长春龙嘉国际机场 http://www.jlairports.com/List/introduce.